Table Manners *for Beginners*

A Civilized Introduction to the Ross Periodic Table

Second Edition

Jim Ross

 London Ontario Canada

National Library of Canada Cataloguing in Publication	Ross, Jim (James William), 1952-
	Table manners for beginners : a civilized introduction to the Ross periodic table
	1. Chemistry, Organic--Textbooks. I. Title.
	QD253.2.R67 2013 547 C2013-901335-X

Author	Jim Ross
Printer	CreateSpace
Cover Design	Jim Ross

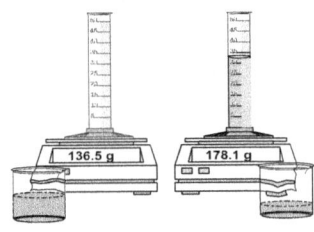

© Copyright 2013 by Ross Lattner Educational Consultants.

All rights reserved. The use of any part of this publication, reproduced, transmitted in any form or by any means, electronic, mechanical, photocopying, recording or otherwise, or stored in a retrieval system, without the prior consent of the publisher, is an infringement of the copyright law and is forbidden.

Permission is granted to the individual teacher who purchases one copy of *Table Manners 2nd Ed.*, to reproduce the student activities for use in his / her classroom only. Reproduction of these materials for an entire school, or for a school system or for other colleagues or for commercial sale is strictly prohibited.

ISBN	978-1-897007-04-4
Offices	London Ontario Canada

To teachers, parents and students everywhere who desire to bring about new ways of understanding the world.

I welcome your comments and suggestions. Let me know what you find most useful.

I've worked hard to remove any errors. Still, don't let a day go by without letting me know if you find one.

Stay in touch.

Jim Ross

Jim Ross
519.639.0412
jim@rosslattner.ca
www.rosslattner.ca
Ross Lattner Educational Consultants
innovative curriculum design
since 1991
147 William Street
London, Ontario
N6B 3B4

rosslattner
Intuitiv CHEMISTRY
chemistry education for all of us

I thank all of the great colleagues
I've had over the years,
in Belleville and in London.
I wish especially to remember Tim Buckley,
a science department head who always,
and jealously,
thought of students first.

Table of Contents

Parents and Teachers Guide and Resource 1

Lab 1.1: The Bohr-Rutherford Model of the Atom 4
Activity 1.2: Organization of the Periodic Table 5
Activity 1.3: Bohr, Rutherford and the Periodic Table. 5
Activity 1.1: Valence Electrons, Atomic Cores and the Periodic Table 6
Activity 1.2: Atomic Radius and the Periodic Table 7
Resource 1.1: The Standard Periodic Table 8
Quiz 1: The Ross Periodic Table 8
Activity 1.3: If you were an electron... where would you go? 10
Activity 1.4: Electronegativity χ 11
Activity 1.5: The Metals 12
Activity 1.6: The Non-Metals 13
Activity 1.7: The Metalloids 14
Activity 1.8: The Noble Gases 15
Quiz 1: The Elements of the Periodic Table 15
Lab 2.1: Reactions of Group 17, Halogens 16
Lab 2.2: Properties of Group 1, the Alkali Metals 18
Lab 2.3: Reactions of the Row Three Elements 20
Lab 2.4: Reactivity of the Noble Gases 22
Activity 4.1: Covalent Bonding 24
Activity 4.2: Polar Covalent Bonds 26
Activity 4.3: Ionic Bonds 28
Lab 4.4: Ionic Solids, Covalent Solids, and Network Solids 30
Activity 4.5: Electron Clouds and Electron Density 32

Table of Contents

Student Exercises and Labs ... 35

Lab 1.1: The Bohr-Rutherford Model of the Atom ... 36
Activity 1.2: Organization of the Periodic Table ... 38
Activity 1.3: Bohr, Rutherford and the Periodic Table ... 40
Activity 1.4: Valence Electrons, Atomic Cores and the Periodic Table ... 42
Activity 1.5: Atomic Radius and the Periodic Table ... 44
Resource 1.6: The Standard Periodic Table ... 46
Quiz 1: The Ross Periodic Table ... 47
Activity 2.1: If you were an electron... where would you go? ... 50
Activity 2.2: Electronegativity ... 52
Activity 2.3: The Metals ... 54
Activity 2.4: The Non-Metals ... 56
Activity 2.5: The Metalloids ... 58
Activity 2.6: The Noble Gases ... 60
Quiz 2: Elements of the Periodic Table ... 61
Lab 3.1: Reactions of Group 17, the Halogens ... 64
Lab 3.2: Reactions of Group 1, the Alkali Metals ... 66
Lab 3.3: Reactions of the Row Three Elements ... 68
Lab 3.4: Reactivity of the Noble Gases ... 70
Quiz 3: Well-Behaved Elements of the Core Valence Radius Table ... 72
Activity 4.1: Covalent Bonds ... 74
Activity 4.2: Polar Covalent Bonds ... 76
Activity 4.3: Ionic Bonds ... 78
Lab 4.4: Ionic Solids, Covalent Solids, and Network Solids ... 80
Activity 4.5: Electron Clouds and Electron Density ... 82
Quiz 4: Covalent, Polar and Ionic Bonding ... 84

The Ross Periodic Table

Parents and Teachers Guide and Resource

There are hundreds of different periodic tables available, and many books about them. So why one more?

The Ross (core - valence - radius) periodic table is *designed for learners*: it helps beginners achieve a deep and dynamic understanding of chemistry right from the start. Why is the Ross table so effective? The Ross table and the related exercises are based upon some of the most robust findings of science education research. Three particular research programs are addressed.

First: This book is compatible with the emerging consensus on the nature of science.

The first, and perhaps the only, goal of science is explanation.

Our curricula ought to look more like science. That is, we ought to require our students to explain the world around them. Too much of our instruction asks the beginning student to explain the science, instead of explaining the world. The periodic table is frequently taught as a thing in need of an explanation, rather than a tool which can help students do the explaining. In this book, the periodic table becomes a powerful explanatory tool in the hands of the beginning chemistry student.

Science is not so much the study of nature itself, as it is the study of humanly constructed *representations* of nature.

Science advances by testing its representations of nature, refining them, and making them more convincing. Students need to experience how scientists do that work. The Ross table provides a simple representation with considerable explanatory and predictive power. The exercises require the student to test those representations in simple experiments, and to revise their representations if needed. An authentic experience of science is incorporated into the chemistry student's earliest activities.

There may not be a "Scientific Method."

We can agree that there is no single procedure that accounts for all of science. Yet we accept the responsibility of teaching something of the "methods of science." Many of these lab exercises follow the PEOE model (predict, explain, observe explain) to provide beginning students the opportunity to *make*, *defend*, and *test* predictions, and then *revise* their representations in response to experiment. If our students can do these four things, they have made some huge gains in the culture of science.

Theories are not mere half-baked ideas that scientists will get right one day.

A theory is the best, the most complete, the most reliable, and the most valuable kind of scientific knowledge. The Particle Theory of matter, for example, is a fundamental set of understandings about the universe, supported by virtually all known experiments, contradicted by none. The Ross table provides a "pretty good" theory that is within the grasp of beginning chemistry students.

Second: *Student cognitive growth is a work in progress. Our science instruction must work with, not against, the students' nature.*

When human beings first encounter novel events, we reason schematically. Only later do we learn to reason about those events formally.

Linguists and cognitive scientists have identified *schematic reasoning* as one of the deepest and simplest ways that humans make sense of the wold. Schematic reasoning is so fundamental to us that we hardly know we are using it. For example, most humans appear to know that more effort provides more results. That's the *Effort Schema*. Dogs, cats and mice use it, too.

Beginners use the *effort schema* to their advantage when they apply it to chemical concentration: more chemical provides greater concentration, and greater concentration provides greater results. On the other hand, beginners are misled by the *effort schema* when they apply it to LeChatelier's principle.

The Ross table anticipates the student's use of schematic reasoning. Students who use the effort schema with the Ross table can make scientifically defensible predictions. Student successes, like rabbits, are prolific when they come in pairs.

Adult humans can keep about seven things going in their heads at one time. Teenagers can manage four or five.

Some cognitive scientists depict brain activity, including thinking, as the wave-like propagation of neuron activity over the surface of the brain. There is some speculation that abstract thinking may involve constructive and destructive interference of such "thought-waves." Perhaps teenagers do not activate as many neurons and connections, and therefore cannot resolve more than four or five waves without losing or confusing them.

In any case, chemistry is a challenge to beginners because of the sheer number of concepts involved. A prudent science teacher will limit the number of variables that the student must entertain.

In the Ross table, variables are limited to three: the core charge, the valence electrons, and the radius of the valence shell. Most students can make excellent judgements about the relative behavior of elements, based upon just those three variables.

A concept's *meaning* is the set of all of the relationships in which the concept participates.

Human beings cannot capture the meaning of a concept merely by reciting a definition. If we defined *sulfur*, for example, as element 16, we might totally miss the point.

With the Ross table, a student can explain the non-metal character, oxidation states, ionic and covalent bonding, dipolarity, enthalpy, acidic behavior, and many other properties of sulfur. That student can learn a very rich set of relationships in which concept *sulfur* participates.

Third: In science, language and learning are linked.

Narrative is a natural language.

Everybody loves a story, and a good storyteller is always in demand. Stories appear to have a structure that corresponds to human thinking. Even young children can figure out how a story should go together. Try this:

Take a simple story, perhaps twenty sentences or so. Cut the story into single sentences with a word processor, and print each sentence on a separate strip of paper. Most kids will assemble a well-written story quite accurately. How do they know how to do that? It certainly isn't a list of rules that they learned at school!

Narrative appears to be the way that we experience ourselves and our world in a social context. Narrative provides the framework for much more complex thinking.

Science writing is a special kind of narrative.

Teenagers' natural storytelling ability is changing slowly into more formal structures. The first order of business in this transformation is the construction of a well formed sentence.

We can think of a single sentence as a very small story. "When the non-metal oxide dissolved in water, it made an acidic solution." In science, that little sentence-story takes on the flavor of science *if it explains a phenomenon*.

To "explain" something is "to give an account" of that thing, in terms of other things that are

- *simpler*
- *more fundamental*
- *more permanent*

than the phenomenon itself.

The Ross table provides three characteristics of atoms: core charge, valence population, and radius. These characteristics are very simple, very fundamental, and very permanent.

A student's growth in scientific literacy requires ever-expanding fluency in creating representations of the world. It is important that teachers provide opportunities to represent the world in different ways. The Ross table supports the growth of student fluency in drawing the atoms, of course. The Ross table also supports students as they learn to create meaningful sentences to explain a wide range of phenomena.

Let's begin.

Parents and Teachers Guide and Resource

Organization of...

An electron is flying around a nucleus at a low energy level

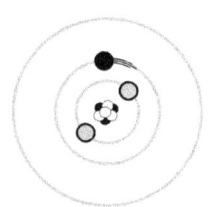

A fast moving particle in the flame collides with the atom, snapping the electron into a higher energy level.

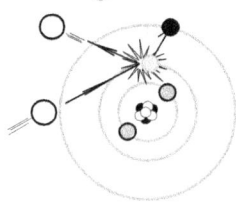

The electron stays briefly in the high energy level.

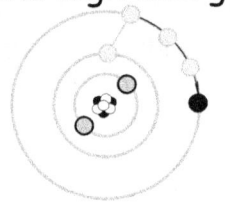

The electron snaps down to the low energy level, giving off energy in the form of light.

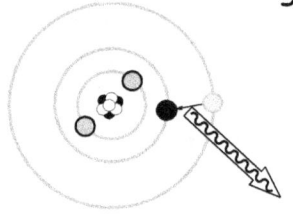

Lab 1.1: The Bohr-Rutherford Model of the Atom

The Learning Activity

1. Place several wooden splints to soak in each of the flasks.
2. It is important that the solutions not become contaminated. Do not mix up the wooden splints.
3. Set up, or show students how to set up, sufficient Bunsen burners. When the flames are hot blue cones,
4. Hold a soaked wooden splint in the flame, and observe the Color produced. Before the wood begins to burn, remove the splint and immerse it in the same solution.
5. Repeat as often as you need to, and make a record of your observations.

Explanation: Once the basic structure of the Bohr-Rutherford model of the atom is sketched out, the narrative at left is a simple extension of the basic model.

Equipment, Preparation and Resources

Nitrates, chlorates, and other oxidizers can accelerate the burning of the wooden splints. Avoid!

Twelve 125 mL Erlenmeyer flasks
Twelve solutions of soluble salts of any of:

Copper	sulfate, chloride, bromide
Lithium	chloride, sulfate
Sodium	chloride, sulfate
Potassium	chloride, sulfate
Strontium	chloride
Barium	chloride

Wooden splints   Bunsen burners
12 stoppers (the solutions can be kept sealed for years)

If the flame is observed through a diffraction grating, the individual colors can be separated. Several images of the flame, one for each Color, will appear in different positions, both to the left and right of the flame itself.

...The Periodic Table

Ideas About Science and Pedagogy

Electrons fill the lowest energy levels first.

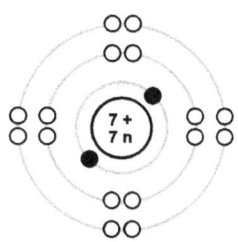

Within any energy level, the first electrons don't pair up, but enter singly and alone.

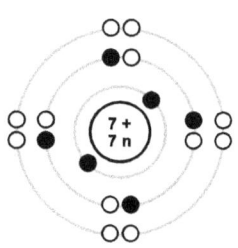

Electrons double up in pairs until that energy level is full.

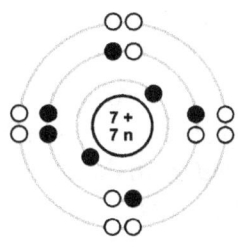

Activity 1.2: Organization of the Periodic Table
Activity 1.3: Bohr, Rutherford and the Periodic Table

Pedagogical Issues The periodic table takes time to learn. Activities 1.2 to 1.6 comprise a series of opportunities to relate atomic structure, group, element name and symbol, atomic number, mass number, valence number, radius, and chemical behavior, including metal, non-metal, and metalloid behavior.

The repetitious application of the Bohr-Rutherford model to the periodic table can do two things. Repetition can reinforce the basic structure of the Bohr-Rutherford model, and allow students to make adjustments to their own learning.

Science Issues We have chosen to use the term "energy level" rather than shell, because of ambiguity in the use of the word "shell" in different popular texts. Second, we have arranged the electrons in pairs, to correspond to the opposite electron spin pairings in the wave mechanical orbital model. Consistent with that model, the electron pair OO corresponds to a single orbital in the wave mechanical model. In accordance with the "aufbau principle" of early quantum mechanics, the electrons should be placed in the lowest energy levels first as singles. When all singles are filled, electrons begin to double up into pairs. The atom at left shows Nitrogen's seven electrons thus arranged.

The Learning Activity In groups or alone, the students complete the atomic number for each position in the table. From the atomic number in its correct position, the number of protons and electrons are determined.

The average atomic mass number indicates the average number of heavy particles in the nucleus. The only heavy particles under normal conditions are protons and neutrons. Since we know the number of protons (the atomic number), the neutrons must make up the difference between the atomic number and the mass number.

Equipment, Preparation and Resources

Pencils, pencil crayons, colored markers

Avoid the use of pen and permanent marker until the basic structure has been worked out.

Organization of...

Parents and Teachers Guide and Resource

The Sodium atom's complete Bohr-Rutherford structure

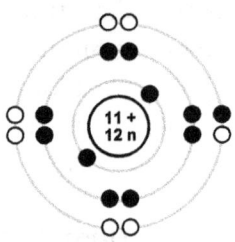

The dotted line divides the valence electrons from the atom's core.

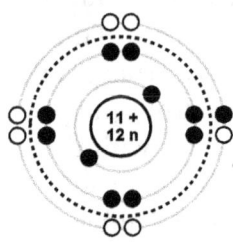

The core contains the nucleus plus completed energy levels. It resembles a noble gas.

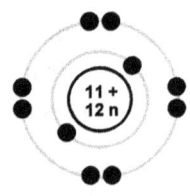

The 10- core electrons plus the 11+ nuclear charge adds up to a total core charge of 1+. The single valence electron moves around the 1+ core.

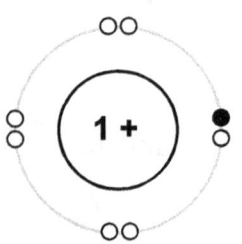

Activity 1.1: Valence Electrons, Atomic Cores and the Periodic Table

Pedagogical Issues This exercise reduces the complexity of the Bohr-Rutherford model, and the introduces two new terms. Prerequisite: the student should be able to use the original Bohr-Rutherford model.

Science Issues The atomic core consists of the nucleus plus the core electrons. The electronic configuration of the core is always that of the previous noble gas, but the nuclear charge is always greater than that of the noble gas. The core electrons can thus be expected to behave like a noble gas, but even more strongly attracted to the nucleus, and therefore even more inert. Since the electrons of the core do not participate in any chemical activity, only the valence electrons and the overall core charge determine the chemical characteristics of the atoms.

The relationship between the core charge, the number of valence electrons, and the periodic table is even simpler and more direct than that of the complete Bohr-Rutherford model. This kind of diagram is readily adaptable to Lewis structures of all kinds.

The Learning Activity
Introduce the idea of the core electrons (much closer to the nucleus than the valence electrons, and much more strongly bound).

Introduce the students to the idea of the atomic core. The atomic core consists of the nucleus plus the core electrons. To students, note that the core charge corresponds to the number of the family or group at the top of the periodic table.

Introduce the student to the idea of the valence electron. Valence electrons (the word "valence" means "fringe" or "edge") are both *farther* from the nucleus and *more shielded* from the nucleus. Thus, the valence electrons can be thought of as being attracted only by the underlying atomic core charge.

Equipment, Preparation and Resources
The student exercises, pencils, pens and markers are all that is required.

© Ross Lattner Publishing   www.rosslattner.ca

...The Periodic Table

Ideas About Science and Pedagogy

A person is about 2 m tall from head to toe.

one thousand times smaller:

A freckle on that person's skin is about 2 mm wide.

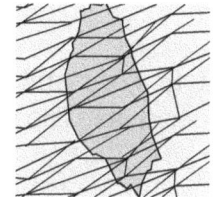

one thousand times smaller:

A skin cell in the freckle might be only 2 μm long.

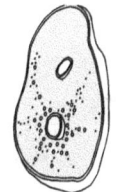

one thousand times smaller:

A cell membrane is about 2 nm, or about 50 atoms wide.

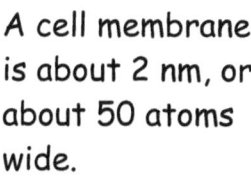

Fifty times smaller:

A single atom is a fraction of a nanometre.

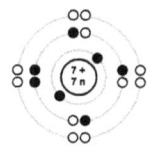

Activity 1.2: Atomic Radius and the Periodic Table

Pedagogical Issues
This activity requires the student to re-present some tabular data in the form of a graph, and then again in pictorial form.

This exercise can become the basis of building physical models of atoms out of play dough. You might wish to have students experiment with steel ball bearings, enclosed in play dough, and surrounded by small magnets. Can you reproduce the behavior of the electrons on those atoms?

Science Issues
Atomic radius is provided in nanometers (10^{-9} m). Most students have not encountered the words picometre (10^{-12} m) or femtometre (10^{-15} m). One nanometre is one millionth of a millimetre. The wavelength of light is often expressed in nanometers (red light is 650 nm).

The Learning Activity
Introduce the students to the idea of atomic radius. One simple scale is in the sidebar at left.

Equipment, Preparation and Resources
pens, pencils, colored markers, student exercise sheets.

Resource 1.1: The Standard Periodic Table

The Ross table is only a portion of the standard table, namely, the s-block and the p-block elements. The students should know that the Ross table presented in this book is a "step on the way" to a more complete understanding of chemical behavior.

One of our goals as chemistry teachers is to enable our students to ever-increasing comprehension of the dynamics of chemical behavior.

To that end, it is important to keep emblems of the whole of chemistry always before the students. The periodic table is surely the most important.

...The Periodic Table

Ideas About Science and Pedagogy

Are there such things as "generic skills" that students can learn in one context and then readily apply them to another context?

Research in learning suggests that the ability to apply a skill or concept in several unrelated contexts is itself a complex ability, and takes time and effort to learn.

It may well be that the skills themselves have no inherent property of "transferability," and that the idea of "generic skills" may be misleading.

Consider a teacher who devotes classroom time and resources teaching one skill to a class. If that teacher expects the students to handily transfer the skill to a new context, both teacher and students are likely to be disappointed.

Quiz 1: The Ross Periodic Table

Pedagogical Issues These tasks are sometimes more complex than they appear. Each one requires a certain level of comprehension, knowledge, and analytical process, so they are not "generic skills" tests as such.

The students' explanations for their answers may be more valuable to you as a teacher than are the answers themselves.

Science Issues These items deal with the students' ability to manipulate various notational forms of the Bohr-Rutherford theory. They also deal with trends in the B-R representations within the periodic table. No mention has been made yet of the chemical behavior of the elements.

The Learning Activity These quizzes can be used profitably in several ways:

Daily Pop Quiz: Did the kids do the homework? Did they understand it? You can pop one of these questions on the class the day after the lesson, and quickly assess problems.

Daily Practice Quiz: If half the class could do it on Tuesday, can they improve by Thursday?

Discussion Generator: Some questions and responses can generate controversy in the classroom. When students are required to explain their beliefs, some very fruitful learning situations can develop.

Question on a later summative test: Use any of these quiz items on a summative test. Students respond more confidently to structures they have seen before.

How Electron Attraction...

Parents and Teachers Guide and Resource

People (and animals) of all ages can rapidly size up a situation and decide who is likely to win and who is likely to lose in an encounter, even if the protagonists have never met before. How do we do this?

Cognitive scientists propose that we use schematic thinking: we rapidly place the situation into a schematic pattern, which then resolves into a very predictable outcome. Magnesium and Oxygen have *different* characteristics among *similar* categories.

The *categories* of the agents are symmetrical (Core, valence, radius)

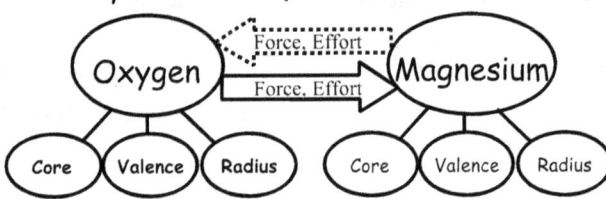

The *struggle* between agents is not symmetrical

In the Ross representation, the categories *core*, *valence* and *radius* have very visible properties. Students can size up those properties, compare the categories, and quickly conclude that oxygen wins electrons, and magnesium loses.

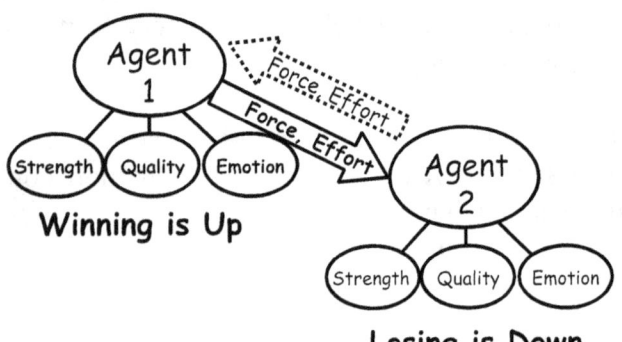

Activity 1.3: If you were an electron... where would you go?

Pedagogical Issues One of the schemata that students tend to use is the *Conflict Schema* (see left). In this activity, we can use students' schematic thinking to great advantage.

If we represent the elements to match the *conflict schema*, students naturally apply the conflict schema to this representation. The students' natural thinking works *for* successful learning scientific concepts.

If teachers representations of atoms do not correspond with student schematic reasoning, then students' natural thinking works *against* scientific concepts; student thinking then appears as a misconception.

Science Issues Whatever our students learn in our introductory chemistry class, we would prefer that their learning never have to be "unlearned" in the future. The Ross schema is essentially correct at this level of resolution. In the future, the student can learn more details which increase the resolution and power of this basic model, but there will be no future need to "unlearn" this model.

The Learning Activity

Students follow a few examples on from the teacher's hand, and then test their judgement on a larger set of exercises.

It is easy to make up more examples for your students, if they are needed.

Equipment, Preparation and Resources

Student exercise pages, pens and pencils.

...Explains Metals and Non-Metals

Ideas About Science and Pedagogy

> Electronegativity is not a fundamental property. It is an aggregate property of an atom, that has been estimated in many different situations.

Activity 1.4: Electronegativity χ

Pedagogical Issues Learning a new scale, not used in everyday life, is a challenge. This scale has been chosen for its ease of learning, not for historical precision. The Row Two elements proceed from 1 to 4 by 0.5 increments. Very simple.

In addition, there is really no pedagogical reason to extend the precision of the scale beyond one decimal place.

Students use electronegativity as a kind of shorthand. The single number summarizes an aggregate of core - valence - radius properties to resolve difficult cases

Science Issues there are several electronegativity scales. All of them propose essentially the same concept, but differ in precise values. The scale used here is an approximation of the scientific scales, and has been chosen for its ease of learning.

Most of the controversies between scales are attempts to resolve some very fine issues about metal / non-metal bonding with ionic or covalent characteristics. In this book, we propose that the ionic / covalent issue is more profitably introduced by comparing the visible metal / non-metal properties of the elements.

In this book, students will use the χ concept in very fruitful ways, but definitely not for the purpose of predicting ionic bonding.

The Learning Activity

Students must have completed Activity 2.1 before this one.

Students will study the electronegativity values in the Ross table, and compare the predictions they made in Activity 2.1 to the predictions they would have made using the χ values.

Equipment, Preparation and Resources

Student exercises, pens and pencils.

Alloys: Solutions of Metals

1. Lead-Free Solder
Traditional solder is 60% Sn and 40% Pb. Modern lead-free solders are 97% Sn and 3% Cu, Bi, Sb, or Ag.

Put the tin into a heavy walled glass test tube, and melt it with a burner flame. Once the tin is liquid, slide a small amount of Bi, Cu, or Ag down the side of the test tube. The tin will quickly dissolve the second metal, producing a shiny metallic alloy.

The alloy can be poured out onto a heat-proof surface such as a concrete or steel slab. This alloy is a common solder.

2. Soldering copper
Clean two pieces of copper tubing and a fitting with steel wool. Apply a thin layer of plumber's flux. Put the two pieces of copper together with the fitting. Heat the fitting with a propane torch. Apply the solder to the joint. The solder will melt and flow wherever the flux has been applied.

When the copper is hot enough to melt the solder, the liquid tin alloy will dissolve the surface of the Cu and form yet another alloy. When the solder cools, the copper pipes will be permanently joined.

3. Pewter.
Modern pewter is 92% tin, 6% antimony and 2% copper. Melts about 290 C. Can be used to cast toys, dishes, etc.

Activity 1.5: The Metals

Pedagogical Issues It's helpful to anchor the students' thinking in a concrete example or two.

Have students make a pendant out of fine copper wire, hang it on some cord or ribbon, and wear it around their neck or wrist for a few days. The properties of a metal are all within view.

Science Issues If we take seriously the idea that science is mostly about explanation, then we ought to explain *why* metals and non-metals behave the way they do. This exercise, and those following, are an attempt to do that.

Virtually all of the bulk properties of metals can be explained by referring to the loosely held cloud of electrons in the metal.

Metals, when mixed, don't react. They simply dissolve in each other to make alloys. As long as the two metals have similar sizes and / or similar electron energy levels, an alloy is easy to form.

The metal cores simply migrate into the cloud of delocalized electrons of the "host" metal. The result is a new metallic solution, often with quite different properties from any of the constituent metals.

The Learning Activity Students test several metals for electrical and thermal conductivity, reflectivity and malleability

Equipment, Preparation and Resources

Thermal conductivity: place the metal against an ice cube.

Electrical conductivity: low voltage conductivity tester.

...Explains Metals and Non-Metals

Ideas About Science and Pedagogy

What do non-metals look like?

Crystalline sulfur is arranged into molecules of 8 sulfur atoms. At low temperatures, sulfur melts into a pale yellow liquid, molecules intact.

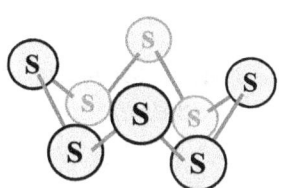

At higher temperatures, the S_8 molecule is broken, and the open rings link to form a chain. The liquid abruptly becomes dark and tarry.

Heated farther, the sulfur becomes very dark, but much less viscous. When poured into ice water, the sulfur is chilled into a long stretchy rubber.

By the next day, the sulfur will revert to its crystalline form.

At no time does sulfur resemble a metal!!

Activity 1.6: The Non-Metals

Pedagogical Issues Non-metals abound in compounds. However, since only a few are common as elements, students are unlikely to have experienced many non-metal elements. Sulfur, carbon, oxygen and nitrogen are the most common non-metal elements. Students may be familiar with the smell of chlorine in swimming pools and bleach. Iodine and hydrogen are available in chemistry labs.

Science Issues The behavior of non metals, whether as elements or as compounds, depends largely upon their great core charges and the subsequent tight binding of valence electrons in small radius atoms.

Whether as elements or as compounds, the non-metals typically form covalent compounds of shared covalent pairs of electrons.

The Learning Activity As before, students examine a number of non-metals, and test them for electrical and thermal conductivity, for reflectivity and for malleability.

Equipment, Preparation and Resources

Thermal conductivity: hold the sample against an ice cube to feel whether heat is rapidly conducted from your hand into the colder ice.

Electrical conductivity: test with a low-voltage conductivity tester.

Reflectivity: visually examine the sample for shiny reflective surface.

Malleability: tap the sample with a small hammer, spoon, or retort rod.

© Ross Lattner Publishing   www.rosslattner.ca

Activity 1.7: The Metalloids

Silicon is easily available as large (1 cm) lumps from chemical supply houses.

Pedagogical Issues Apart from silicone, most students have no experience with this element.

Silicon is shiny like a metal.

Science Issues

Silicon is a modest conductor of heat and electricity

Silicon's midway point between metal and non-metal behaviour makes it invaluable as a semi-conductor.

Silicon is very brittle, like a non-metal (at least, certainly *not* like a metal).

As a pure element, silicon is a very poor conductor indeed. Carefully mixed with very tiny amounts of other elements, silicon can be made to conduct a current.

The Learning Activity

Finally, silicon is hard enough to easily scratch glass.

Three elements will be tested as before: sulfur, silicon and aluminum. Since S and Al have been tested previously, the purpose is to differentiate Si from both metals and non-metals.

So.. Is silicon a metal, or a non-metal? Or something else?

Equipment, Preparation and Resources

Low- voltage conductivity tester

Ice cube to test thermal conductivity

...Explains Metals and Non-Metals

Ideas About Science and Pedagogy

Can teachers legitimately speak of a "stable octet," when they are aware of all of the following well-known chemistry facts?

- Xe, Kr and even Ar break that "stable octet" to make compounds. Furthermore, the reactions are exothermic!

- covalent Xe, Kr and Ar compounds are stable in vacuum, yet all have more than 8 valence electrons!

- Many stable covalent compounds have more or less than 8 valence electrons.

- For an atom, both gaining and losing electrons to achieve an octet is an endothermic (unstable) process.

NO! The idea that elements "want a stable

Activity 1.8: The Noble Gases

Pedagogical Issues The patterns established in the previous pages prevail in the noble gases as well. To introduce the (false) concept of the "stable octet" would be bad pedagogy. There is no special stability to having 8 electrons. Atoms can't count, so why do they "want" 8 electrons? To break the Ross pattern in favor of a special "stable octet" status for the noble gases would break the whole pattern that our students have been striving to learn.

Science Issues A common definition of the valence shell contains these words: " the valence shell is a partially filled shell." If this definition is used in conjunction with the "stable octet" concept, students will think that the outermost electrons in a noble gas are not valence electrons. In the Ross model, the outermost shell of a noble gas is simply the full valence shell! The valence shell has 8 electrons in it, and the core charge is +8

The Learning Activity is a brief pencil and paper activity with the student work sheets.

Quiz 1: The Elements of the Periodic Table

Pedagogical Issues "Kids don't learn what goes in through their senses. They learn what comes out of them, through their expression."

Is that an exaggeration? Think of this. Each day, perhaps a million events enter our brains through our senses, yet most of them fade from memory, never to be recalled again. One of the remarkable features of the human brain is precisely its ability to "lose" memories. Imagine what our minds would be like if our brains remembered every detail that entered our senses! So merely *reading* the Ross table is not likely to result in learning.

On the other hand, when we repeat deliberate movements, our actions are rapidly learned as skills. The more practice we have, the more likely it is that we will learn the new skill. So... study of the Ross table should be *practice using the Ross table*! That practice is what these quizzes provide.

Parents and Teachers Guide and Resource

Chemical Groups...

The *Effort* schema is a small fragment of everyday thinking that students use to make sense of the world.

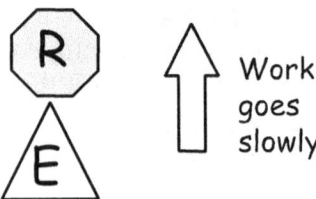

Work goes slowly

E stands for Effort, R for Resistance. Most students are very certain that doubling E will always double the results.

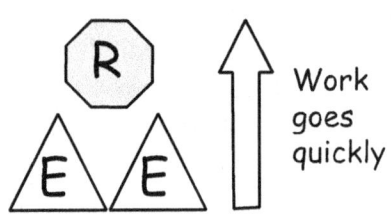

Work goes quickly

In this lab, a student might conceive of the bromine as exerting effort upon a resistive dye particle.

If bromine reacts faster than iodine, students mentally reorganize the phenomenon of reaction rate into something like "bromine has a stronger attraction than iodine"

Lab 2.1: Reactions of Group 17, Halogens

Pedagogical Issues Our teaching objective is to have students relate the small radius of the halogens to their ability to attract and hold electrons from other atoms. The smaller the radius, the more able to attract electrons. The core charge and valence values are the same in the halogens, so they are not compared. The success of this demonstration depends upon students observing greater rate of reaction with the smaller halogens. Unconsciously using *Effort* schema, students will generally associate the fastest rate with the greatest ability to attract and hold electrons. The greater the effort, the greater the results.

Science Issues The phenomenon of *bleaching* almost always involves oxidation of a colored compound. For example, the dye molecules in a photograph have extended, conjugated double bond systems. Each double bond contains a pair of π electrons, which bromine can easily remove. Once the double bond system is gone, the molecule can no longer interact with light at the particular frequency that gives the dye its characteristic color.

While we would predict the rates chlorine > bromine > iodine in oxidative ability, in fact this is not the case in oxidation of organic dyes. Bromine is a faster bleaching agent than chlorine. Perhaps bromine's size may be a better match to the C=C double bond. ***For both safety and pedagogical reasons, don't use chlorine for the bleaching experiment. Compare bromine and iodine only.***

Because rates are very sensitive to temperature and concentration, all solutions should be around 15°C. To prepare fresh solutions at approximately equal concentrations, see instructions opposite.

A color photo is the best dye to bleach. Any colored cotton or paper product will work, but more slowly. Experiment with a piece of blue denim, an old playing card, comic strips, maps, etc.

These chemicals are immediately noxious. Use the fume hood! Safety goggles at all times, and small quantities only.

Other experiments: How quickly do these solutions oxidize a ball of fine copper wire, or other metals such as aluminum or iron?

...and Chemical Behavior

Ideas About Science and Pedagogy

Label three clean dry 500 mL flasks Cl, Br, and I. Put 3 g KBr into flask Br, and 4 g KI into flask I.

Just before use, put 25 mL of bleach into each flask.

To each flask add 450 mL of 0.1 M HCl (Hydrochloric acid).

Caution: the acid will generate free chlorine gas. The Cl_2 gas will displace Br_2 and I_2.

Categories:
Knowledge:
Inquiry:
Communication:

The Learning Activity Teacher Demonstration. This lab contains too many chemical hazards for kids.
Before the experiment
   Predict: Which halogen will be the most reactive bleaching agent... bromine, or iodine?
   Explain prediction, using both valence - core diagrams, and sentences.

Once the solutions are prepared, place strips of a photograph in the solution, leave for a few seconds, and remove and rinse in warm water. Examine the specimens for bleaching.

After the experiment
   Observe and make records of your observations.
   Explain prediction, using both valence - core diagrams,

Equipment, Preparation and Resources Solutions of halogens in water are available, but even when fresh, their concentrations are different. Once opened, their concentrations change rapidly, and there is no simple way to measure and adjust them. You can get around the problem by preparing solutions from liquid chlorine bleach, which is about 5% NaClO by mass. You need the chlorine to generate bromine and iodine. You do not need chlorine for the demonstration.

Caution: Work in a fume hood! The resulting solutions will be 0.035 M Cl_2, Br_2 and I_2. The total volume of Cl_2 gas released will be 400 mL over a period of several hours. The Bromine will disperse more slowly, and the Iodine over a period of days.

$$2\ HCl + NaClO \Rightarrow H_2O + NaCl + Cl_2$$

$$Cl_2 + 2\ KBr \Rightarrow 2\ KCl + Br_2$$

$$Cl_2 + 2\ KI \Rightarrow 2\ KCl + I_2$$

Assessment and Evaluation
Questions for Later
Generation of new questions

Should our society use large amounts of chlorine?

Chemical Groups...

Parents and Teachers Guide and Resource

When students cannot understand the dynamics of a situation, they often use the *Conflict* schema to organize objects into "winners" and "losers." These roles have strong emotional meanings; students find them very convincing.

The struggle between agents is not symmetrical

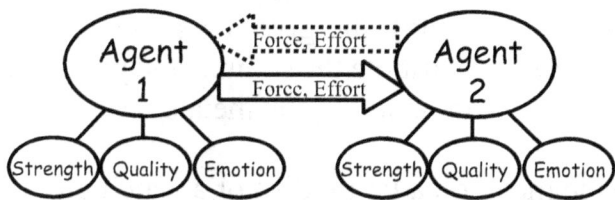

The categories of the agents are symmetrical

When water and sodium interact, students tend to mentally organize them as if Na and H₂O were locked in a *Conflict*:

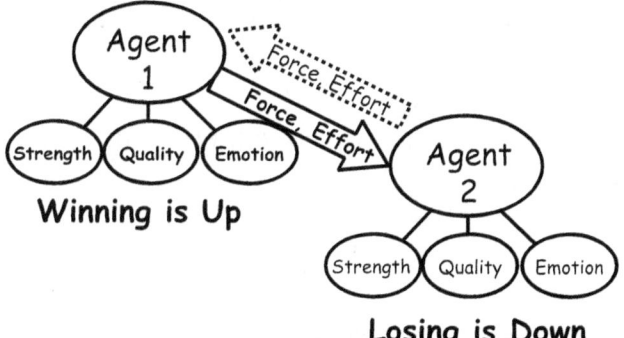

Winning is Up

Losing is Down

Listen for student use of words that indicate struggle: *take over, win or lose, stronger or weaker, can't resist.* These may indicate non-scientific modes of thinking that actually oppose learning of scientific explanation.

Lab 2.2: Properties of Group 1, the Alkali Metals

Pedagogical Issues Who is acting upon whom? We would like to see the students to "see" that water (hydrogen in the water, actually) can easily remove electrons from the alkali metals. The student, on the other hand, "sees" an exotic metal touching an ordinary glass of drinking water, then sparking and popping. The student is likely to think that the sodium is doing something to the water.

One of our pedagogical tasks here is to cast the water (or the hydrogen in the water) in the role of the *agent*. It is the water that attracts the electrons of the alkali metals. If we are successful, the problem now looks like an equal effort (water) acting upon an unequal resistance (the alkali metals).

Science Issues Once again, the key issue is safety. The metals react very quickly with water, generating hydrogen gas and often igniting it with the heat of reaction. The hydrogen can occasionally pop. Safety goggles, larger beakers, and wire gauze reduce the hazard.

As lithium reacts slowly with water, it should be the first metal the students work with.

Cut the metals carefully into 2 mm cubes, just before the experiment. If holes are poked in the metal, or an oxide crust is permitted to form around the metal, then explosions occasionally happen. Smooth, clean metal samples generally react smoothly.

An alternative is to use a video of the demonstration.

...and Chemical Behavior

Ideas About Science and Pedagogy

Students should make their initial predictions and explanations the night before the experiment.

When a student encounters something new, he or she will usually resort to schematic thinking first. Such a student might say "sodium is stronger than water", or "potassium is stronger than sodium."

Teachers cannot eliminate schematic thinking, nor should we try. We need to *re-present* the problem so that student schematic thinking supports science.

The Ross model confines student attention to three features: core charge, valence electrons and radius. Natural schematic thinking "works" with these features to support a scientific explanation:

"Hydrogen and sodium have the same core charge. Hydrogen has a much smaller radius. Electrons are more attracted to hydrogen than to sodium."

The Learning Activity Go over all of the instructions, emphasis on clean, dry work place.

Before the experiment
    Predict which alkali metal will be most reactive with water
    Explain the prediction, using core - valence diagrams and complete sentences

When all preparations are made (goggles on, beaker with water, tongs, wire gauze ready), the give the students small portions of lithium. Only distribute the sodium and potassium as they gain experience with handling the metals.

Students receive the metal on a Petrie dish or a watch glass to take back to their desk, and handle the metal only with tongs. As soon as they have put the metal into the water, they must cover the beaker with the wire gauze in order to prevent spattering.

After the experiment

    Observe the reactivity of the alkali metals, and record.
    Explain observations, using core - valence diagrams and complete sentences.

Students should use fresh water for each experiment. This is important for comparison.

Equipment, Preparation and Resources

Goggles at all times. Standard student lab kit, including beakers, wire gauze, tongs, watch glass.

Handle the metals cautiously with tongs. Carefully blot up as much of the paraffin as you can. Do not touch the metal with your bare skin. Cut the metals with a sharp knife or scalpel into pieces about 2mm × 2mm × 2mm. Err on the small side.

You can replace the lab with a demonstration or even a video.

Chemical Groups...

Parents and Teachers Guide and Resource

If you were an electron ●, where would you rather be?

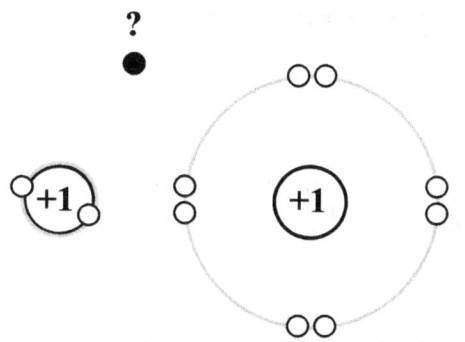

six paces from +1 Na, or one pace from +1 H ?

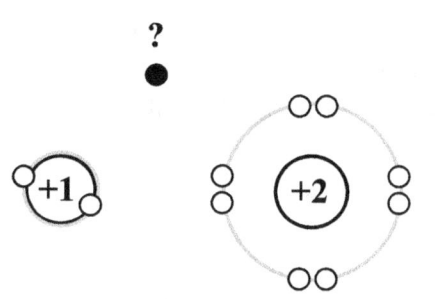

Will the electron tend to stay four paces from +2 Mg or one pace from +1 H ?

Lab 2.3: Reactions of the Row Three Elements

Pedagogical Issues Two intellectual tasks are required of the student in this lab. First, the student must provide some representation of the trends in the visible chemical behaviors of the row three elements. Second, the student must provide an explanation for those phenomena.
The only samples studied in this series are the first four elements of the row. A student could be expected to see the trend among those elements, but not the remaining elements in the series.

Science Issues The explanation for the trend of activity among the first four elements should contain references to the trends in the size of the core charge, and the radius of the atoms. In general, the greater the core charge, the more tightly the electrons are held; the smaller the radius, the more tightly the electrons are held.

One of the practical problems with labs of this type is the difficulty of actually comparing oranges with oranges. Sodium, magnesium and aluminum are all metallic solids. Silicon is not entirely metallic; at least some of its hard, diamond-like character appears to be related to covalent network structure.

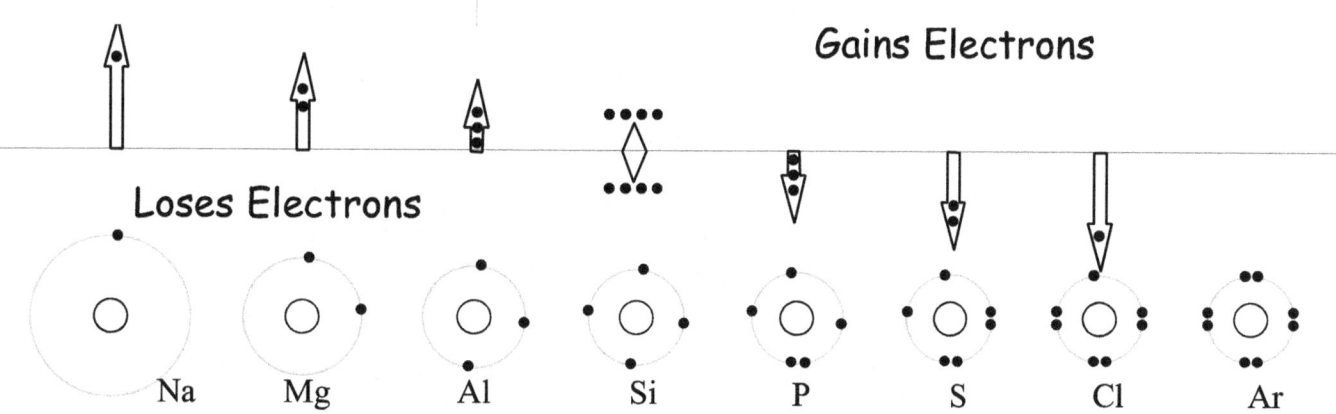

Fill in the core charge for each element. The length of the arrow indicates how readily the electrons are lost or gained. Silicon can either lose or gain electrons, but does neither readily. Argon strongly attracts its own electrons, but its valence shell is completely full, so it cannot hold electrons from other atoms.

© Ross Lattner Publishing   www.rosslattner.ca

...and Chemical Behavior

Ideas About Science and Pedagogy

The Learning Activity

Students are to prepare four small 100 mL beakers with 50 mL of cold water, and have ready a wire gauze and tongs.

Before the experiment

> **Predict** the order of activity with water, from most reactive to least reactive. Then, **Predict** the order of activity with acid.
> **Explain** predictions, using the valence - core diagrams and complete sentences.

Students are given small samples of silicon, aluminum, magnesium, and sodium., which they add to the water. The Sodium reacts vigorously as before; Magnesium may show some tiny bubbles; the others appear inert.

Only Mg, Al, and Si remain for the second part. The students pour off the water, and replace it with 0.5 M HCl. The Mg reacts vigorously, Al reacts slowly but releases much heat, and the Silicon reacts not at all.

After the experiment

> **Observe** the reactivity of the row three elements with water and with acid, and record your observations here
> **Explain** observations, using core - valence diagrams, and complete sentences.

Equipment, Preparation and Resources

0.5 M HCl	Pour 40 mL of conc. HCl into 500 ml cold water. Add water to make 1 L.
Na	Cut into 2mm cubes as before
Mg	Cut Mg ribbon into 3 cm strips
Al	Strips of Al foil, about 1 cm × 3 cm.
Si	Small crystals. These are quite inert, and should be collected, washed, and kept for next year.

Caution: When aluminum reacts with HCl, it produces a great deal of heat. The increasing temperature can result in a fast reaction rate.

Chemical Groups...

Parents and Teachers Guide and Resource

W tungsten

Ar argon   O oxygen

Tungsten VI oxide, the product of this reaction, is generally regarded as safe.

Enclose the bulb, pliers, and a heavy file inside a double plastic bag. From the outside, move the file to scratch the bulb, then break the glass.

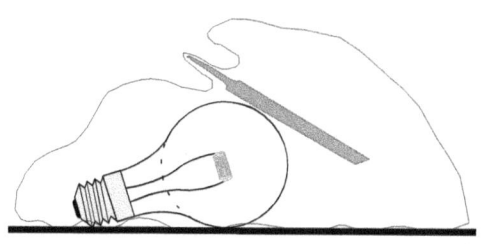

Remove glass with pliers. Be careful not to break the tungsten filament.

Lab 2.4: Reactivity of the Noble Gases

Pedagogical Issues First, how do you demonstrate inert behavior? By definition, nothing happens. The strategy in this lab is to show that tungsten reacts readily with one common gas, oxygen, but tungsten does not react with the inert gas, argon.

Second: how do you explain inert behavior as an active phenomenon? Students are likely to accept an explanation that corresponds to their own schematic thinking structures.

Argon, with a core charge of +8 and a small radius, will strongly attract valence electrons. Argon also has a full valence shell, which will block the acquisition of more electrons. A strong "effort" is matched by a strong "block." Nothing happens.

Science Issues The most common way to treat the noble gases in textbooks is to speak of a "stable octet." This is an account in need of an explanation! Why, exactly, is an octet stable? What, in fact, is meant by "stable?" Are octets inherently stable? How do atoms know that they have octets?

The "octet rule" is simply not useful as an explanatory model. It should be dropped in favor of the a more powerful Ross model.

For its part, the tungsten itself is not a main block element, but a transition metal. When we assign a core charge of +6, we are looking at its maximum (and commonest) oxidation state of +6. Its radius has been taken from common tables.

Tungsten is not particularly reactive, and does ignite only at very high temperatures achieved when an electric current passes through the filament.

The product, WO_3 is generally regarded as safe, but it is enclosed in a beaker to reduce exposure and to sequester the product for later examination.

© Ross Lattner Publishing   www.rosslattner.ca

...and Chemical Behavior

Ideas About Science and Pedagogy

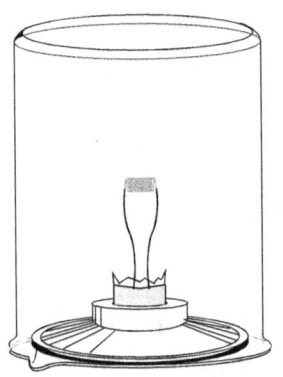

Turn the bulb on for a few seconds. The tungsten will ignite, and burn with a bright flame, much like Mg.

The Learning Activity

Before the experiment

Predict: Students know how the tungsten filament behaves in argon. What will happen in oxygen?
Explain: Students must draw diagrams, write sentences.

After the Experiment

Observe and make records of the experiment.
Explain the observations using Ross diagrams and sentences.

Equipment, Preparation and Resources

several 100 W bulbs   safe light bulb sockets
file   needle nose pliers
plastic bags   2 L beaker

Parents and Teachers Guide and Resource

How the Ross Model...

Caution: This is the place that the "stable octet" concept provides the greatest danger to the learner!

1. Fluorine is unable to count. How can it know if it has an octet, stable or not?

2. Fluorine has no emotions, and cannot "want" anything.

3. Fluorine cannot intend anything, let alone an octet.

4. Exactly why is one extra electron unstable?

5. See (2) above

6. See (3) above

7. Losing an electron is an endothermic process, and sodium is unable to "want" it to be otherwise.

8. For the element F_2 gas to acquire two electrons is a very endothermic process, not at all spontaneous.

9. There really is no such thing as a single "ionic bond." Ionic compounds are formed as large-scale crystal structures.

Activity 4.1: Covalent Bonding

Science Issues Chemical bonding has usually been taught from the Bohr-Rutherford framework, and often represented by Lewis dot diagrams.

Under those two representations, the general approach has been to deal with the ionic bond first, the covalent bond second, and finally the polar covalent bond. This has established ionic bonds as the prototypical bond in the minds of most students. Perhaps the ionic bond occupies a pre-eminent place of privilege in many teachers' minds as well.

Under that paradigm, the chemical dynamic has been pictured something like this:

1. "Fluorine does not have a stable octet."
2. "Fluorine wants a stable octet."
3. "Fluorine will take an electron in order to achieve a stable octet."

4. "Sodium has one extra electron, beyond a stable octet."
5. "Sodium wants a stable octet."
6. "Sodium will lose its extra electron to achieve a stable octet."

7. "Sodium loses its electron, becoming a 1+ sodium ion."
8. "Fluorine gains an electron, becoming a 1– fluoride ion."
9. "The two ions attract each other, forming an ionic bond."

Each of these statements can be refuted. See left.

When students use the Ross diagram and their schematic reasoning, they make much better progress by starting at the covalent bond.

First, students can intuitively understand the underlying dynamic of the bonding process.

Second, every claim made using the Ross diagram also supported by (almost) all other, more comprehensive, models of the atom.

© Ross Lattner Publishing   25   www.rosslattner.ca

...Explains Chemical Bonding

Ideas About Science and Pedagogy

We live in a graphical world, a world of images. One feature of images is that **images cannot dialogue.**

Images alone are insufficient to provide dialogue. Perhaps this contributes to our society's increasingly centrifugal dynamic. The center cannot hold. Politics become divisive.

In the science classroom, the images of atoms forming covalent bonds are, by themselves, insufficient for student understanding.

Understanding requires students to enter into explanatory dialogues with each other. This means: **students must be required to tell the story of their diagrams using well-formed sentences.**

Now consider each of these arguments:

1. Notice the unpaired valence electron on the valence of the fluorine atom.
2. Non-metals like fluorine have large core charges and small radii.
3. Fluorine's valence electrons are strongly attracted to its atomic core.
4. How could the unpaired electron be even more strongly attracted?
5. If it occupied the vacancy on a second fluorine atom, it could be attracted to *two* 7+ core charges!
6. Both unpaired electrons now occupy this doubly attracted state, and neither fluorine atom has any vacancies.
7. Voila! A covalent bond.

Pedagogical Issues A student, using just a Ross representation of two fluorine atoms, can construct a narrative account of the covalent bond in terms of things that are simpler, more fundamental, and more permanent than the covalent bond itself. In other words, the student can provide a scientific explanation of the covalent bound.

The schematic nature of the student's reasoning will continue to provide insights into other chemical reactions into which the fluorine molecule might enter. This provides very robust learning, without resorting to the indefensible fictions of the traditional paradigm.

The Learning Activity

1. Draw each atom alone, before it forms any bonds.
2. Identify the unpaired electrons.
3. Draw an arrow on each unpaired electron, pointing toward its "home" core charge. Make the arrow in centimetres, the same length as the electronegativity. , and the vacancies on each atom.
4. Draw the atoms adjacent to each other, with the previously unpaired electrons now being attracted to both core charges.
5. Draw the arrows, showing each bonding electron attracted to two core charges.

The conflict schema.

Activity 4.2: Polar Covalent Bonds

Pedagogical Issues The notion of a *polar covalent bond* lies utterly outside your students' experience. It is an abstraction without an experience.

Teachers have two avenues of organizing student experiences of this concept.

1. The student can experience the muscles and nerves in their hands and eyes as they draw diagrams of polar covalent bonds. Students can experience the mental and emotional activity as they plan each small line and dot in the diagram. Because the students use their schematic reasoning as they plan and draw, the experience of drawing is a very dynamic series of events.

2. The student can experience physical events that provide indirect evidence of polar covalent bonding, such as melting point, boiling point and solubility interactions. If these experiences are to make sense, they must reflect the experience of drawing.

3. Merely watching a video is insufficient. The student can go through numerous "I see it, I recognize it" cycles, and not be able to reproduce it. This phenomenon is often called "lack of retention," but its roots are in the low level of experience, and the illusory emotional response, that video provides.

Science Issues There are two parts to the phenomenon of bond polarity. The first part is the different strength of attraction that the core charge exerts on the electrons. The second part is the degree to which the positions of the electrons are shifted from a perfectly non-polar equilibrium.

By appealing to electronegativity, this activity can deal convincingly with different attractions. It has very little to say about the displacement of electrons. For a related account of electron displacement, see *Activity 4.5: Electron Clouds and Electron Density*.

...Explains Chemical Bonding

Ideas About Science and Pedagogy

Electronegativity is not a fundamental property of atoms. It is an aggregate property, a relative property, a property that must be estimated over many different situations.

Many introductory chemistry courses insist that "a difference in χ greater than 1.70 predicts ionic bonding." Is that true?

The rule of 1.7 would predict that PF_3 is ionic, and $AlBr_3$ is covalent. Wrong on both counts.

Students can actually predict the ionic / covalent properties of these compounds more accurately by comparing visible properties of the elements.

Can electronegativity be used to accurately predict covalent and ionic behavior of chemical compounds of

The Learning Activity

1. Draw each atom alone, before it forms any bonds.
2. Identify the unpaired electrons.
3. Draw an arrow on each unpaired electron, pointing toward its "home" core charge. Make the arrow in centimetres, the same length as the electronegativity. , and the vacancies on each atom.
4. Draw the atoms adjacent to each other, with the previously unpaired electrons now being attracted to both core charges.
5. Draw the arrows, showing each bonding electron attracted to two core charges.

Equipment, Preparation and Resources

Student exercise pages, pens, pecils, and rulers

When it comes to the issue of student experience, we have inherited a problem from the nineteenth century.

A traditional, nineteenth century approach to science suggests that the young scientist must observe a wide variety of phenomena, and then infer an explanation.

There are some big problems with this.

First, classroom teachers cannot provide students with the sheer number of "ionic experiences" that they would need.

Second, there are no "rules of inference." Teachers really have no "method of inference" to teach students.

It is much more fruitful to provide students with a good working model.

Then the student can test the model against a small number of experiences.

Activity 4.3: Ionic Bonds

Pedagogical Issues We return to the issue of student experience.

Students have had thousands of experiences with metals and non-metals. By there experiences alone, students can easily identify metals. Once they learn their properties, students can usually identify non-metallic elements. All of this can be reinforced by providing the student with experiences of metals and non-metals, and by requiring them to explain the origin of those behaviors.

Student experiences with ionic solids are not as well-defined. It is up to chemistry teachers to provide those experiences. In order to advance student learning, we have can do three things:

1. Make students aware that this stuff that they are experiencing is an ionic solid.
2. Require students to make representations of ionic bonding, and ionic solids. The student experience is of a different order: nerves, bones, muscles, eyes, and the mind that plans, executes, and experiences satisfaction, or even delight!
3. Require students to make written and spoken representations of the formation of an ionic bond, using complete grammatical sentences. This, too, is an experience.

Science Issues The "ionic bond" may not actually exist as such. Ionic solids are large-scale crystalline structures, in which oppositely charged ions attract each other into regular arrays. When we represent a single "ionic bond" we are representing an abstract, idealized version of a chemical interaction.

To understand why ionic bonding happens, imagine sodium and fluorine forming a covalent bond.

This is a very unlikely covalent bond. The bonding pair is very weakly attracted to the sodium core. But that means that the sodium core is very weakly attracted to the rest of the system. This would be a large and fragile molecule.

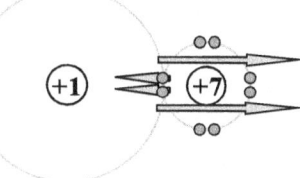

There is a better way.

...Explains Chemical Bonding

Ideas About Science and Pedagogy

Many introductory chemistry courses insist that "a difference in x greater than 1.70 predicts ionic bonding." Is that true?

The "rule of 1.7" would predict that PF_3 is ionic, and $AlBr_3$ is covalent. Wrong on both counts.

Students can actually predict the ionic / covalent properties of these compounds more accurately by comparing visible properties of the elements.

When two elements have obviously metallic and non-metallic appearances to the eye, those two elements will almost certainly react to form an ionic solid.

Can electronegativity be used to accurately predict covalent and ionic behavior of chemical compounds of elements?

Judge for yourself! Then answer the question... why would we want to teach a "rule" that has so many exceptions?

The Learning Activity

Using the Ross models of sodium and fluorine, we can represent the following dynamic.

1. The sodium atom has one electron, orbiting at a large distance from a weak core charge. It is not strongly attracted to the core.
2. The fluorine atom has one vacancy in its valence shell, close to its very strong core charge.
3. The fluorine atom's attraction for electrons is so strong that it "takes custody" of the sodium atom's electron

4. When it loses its valence electron, the sodium atom's valence shell just disappears. If there are no electrons in it, it's not there.

5. The sodium atomic core is the sodium ion.
6. The two oppositely charged ions attract each other.
7. Together, billions of other ions form a large ionic crystal
8. Note: the electrons and atomic cores are closer under ionic bonding than they would have been under covalent bonding.

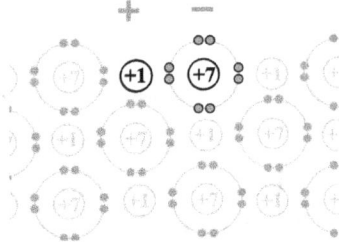

© Ross Lattner Publishing   www.rosslattner.ca

Parents and Teachers Guide and Resource

How the Ross Model...

The Particle Theory of Matter.

First encountered formally at about Grade 7, this theory is foundational. It cannot receive too much exposure.

The absence of matter is a pure vacuum.

All matter is made of tiny particles.

All particles of one substance are identical.

The spaces between particles are small in solids and in liquids, and large in gases.

All particles are attracted to each other by forces.

Particles are in constant motion.

Remind the students that they may need to refer to this simple and powerful theory to explain the behavior of the molecular solids.

Lab 4.4: Ionic Solids, Molecular Solids, and Network Solids

Pedagogical Issues

Once again, experience is the issue here.

Students have a strong intuitive understanding of the category "solid." They do not have distinct classes of experiences of different kinds of solids.

This is especially important because the most commonly experienced solids are the components of the human body, household goods, and the plants and animals experienced in natural settings.

This is a problem, because the vast majority of living things, and materials made from living things, are network solids. Hair, skin, wood, leather, plant and animal fibres, are all natural polymers, and can be grouped together as network solids.

The oils, sugars, flavors and scents produced by plants are best understood as small covalently bonded molecules

The experience of ionicly bonded substances is largely confined to salt, baking soda, epsom salts, and some powdered household laundry detergents.

Science Issues Covalent bonds can hold atoms together over a wide variety of scales. Covalently bonded molecules contain only two atoms to a hundred or so. Network solids can consist of millions of atoms bound together.

Before studying chemistry, the most widely used theory for students is the particle theory of matter.

If the students understand that covalently bonded substances can be small particles, then they can apply the particle theory to the molecules.

...Explains Chemical Bonding

Ideas About Science and Pedagogy

One of the enduring ideas of the nineteenth century is the concept of the "molecule."

The concept has evolved over the past century.

While it was initially used to describe the smallest particle of any kind of substance, that definition ran into trouble.

Today, the most common understanding of the concept of a molecule is:

"A molecule is a discrete particle held together by covalent bonds."

Thus, covalent solids can be thought of as collections of identical particles.

That means that the students can use the particle theory from earlier learning to describe the events in this lab exercise.

The Learning Activity

The student are to systematically apply four tests to seven different substances.

The first five substances are known as ionic solids, covalent solids, or network solids.

Be sure to choose substances that are generally regarded as safe, preferably things that the students would have encountered before.

The n

After the lab:

The two unknown solids are to be judged by the students, by means of the results of the tests.

Equipment, Preparation and Resources

hot plate for 4 students

Molecular solids:
menthol, camphor, peppermint oil, olive oil, paraffin wax, beeswax, sugar

Ionic solids:
drywall, chalk, marble, epsom salts, baking soda

Network solids: silicon, graphite, diamond, quartz, glass, hair, silicone baking implements

How the Ross Model...

Parents and Teachers Guide and Resource

Quantum mechanics is quite possibly the most successful theory devised by human beings.

Of course, QM is very difficult to learn and to teach. There is, however, an experiential part of QM that is accessible by the student: the idea of probability.

In quantum mechanics, the electrons are described as waves. Take a step back, and the electron-waves are represented as wave equations, Ψ.

The probability of actually encountering an electron at any given position is probability P, where:

$$P = \Psi^2$$

Students can represent the electron's probabilistic wandering with a wave-like line. If the student imagines the electron wandering around long enough, leaving a trail behind it, the student can get an idea where the electron spends most of its time.

Activity 4.5: Electron Clouds and Electron Density

Pedagogical Issues

How can a student imagine the unimaginable?

Students know well enough how a particle might behave if it was orbiting a strong or weak attractive field. Slow and loopy meandering for a weak field; tight and rapid orbits for a strong field.

The same thing goes for proximity. A particle close to an attractive centre will orbit quickly. The same particle, far from the same center, will orbit much more slowly.

Most important, a particle that is attracted by two centres will tend to whiz around more frequently in that very attractive region.

Once again, we teachers can use a student's natural playfulness, and schematic understanding, to predict a game-like pattern of behavior.

Science Issues

Electron density is generally greater:

1. closer to the core
2. between two bonded atoms
3. and closer to the most attractive atom (large core charge, small radius)

This is generally true, but in the more detailed QM analysis, there are nodes, lobes, etc.

This is not an insurmountable problem. I have found that my students, having played in this way with circular orbits, are quite happy to do something similar for **p** orbitals, **σ** and **π** orbitals.

The effect is quite profitable in understanding the bonding of organic molecules.

...Explains Chemical Bonding

Ideas About Science and Pedagogy

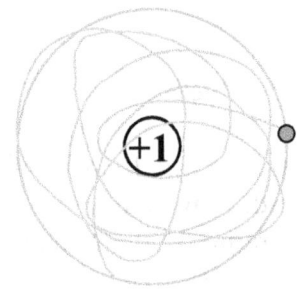

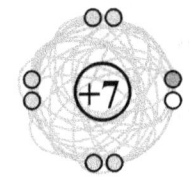

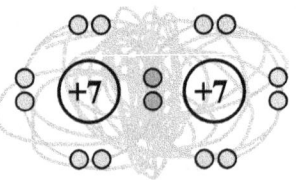

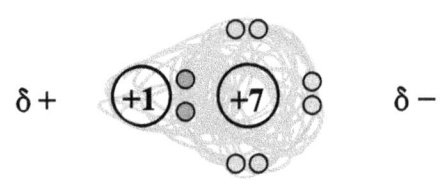

δ+   δ−

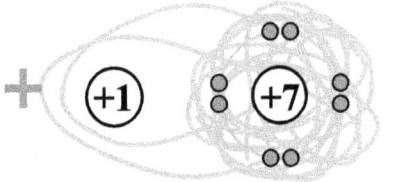

+   −

With a little playfulness, the student can make a "pretty good" picture of electron density.

And electron density is analogous to probability.

The Learning Activity

The student follows this general procedure. It is provided here in more detail so that you can try it out, and then demonstrate it.

1. Draw a line for sodium first.
2. Then try chlorine.
3. Place your pencil on one electron.
4. Move your pencil slowly, so that it loops out ward to valence radius, or even a little beyond it.
5. Continue the line as the electron "falls" into the region between the two atoms, where it is most strongly attracted.
6. As the electron moves outward, it slows down, like a ball thrown into the air.
7. As the electron moves inward, it speeds up, like a falling stone.
8. Continues as if the electron never really hits anything,
9. The more loops you draw, the more the overall picture builds up.
10. Quit when you have a convincing representation.

Equipment, Preparation and Resources

Student exercises, pencils.

Table Manners

Student Exercises and Labs

Knowledge and Understanding

You will learn to use pictures to represent things that you cannot see. Your pictures, even though they may not be scientifically complete, can help you think clearly about the things you can see in your experiments. In particular, you will learn how do draw diagrams of atoms including their atomic cores, valence electrons, and radius..

Knowledge and understanding are probed at regular intervals in the *How Good Are Your Table Manners?* quizzes. Study these as you go through the exercises, so that you can do your best when they are assigned.

Inquiry and Thinking

We will use the PEOE (Predict Explain Observe Explain) cycle for most labs and activities. You are expected to frame a question, provide your best prediction, and explain your thinking, using both sentences and diagrams.

At the end of the unit, you should be able to use the Ross representation of the atom to help you construct good questions and hypotheses about many everyday events.

Communication

The quality of your arguments is the most important aspect of communication in this chapter. Your arguments consist of sentences, organized into paragraphs, and supported by diagrams or other representations.

Each sentence should be clear and to the point. You will find it best to limit your sentences to two concepts linked together to make a reasonable claim. If you need to relate more than two concepts, add a new sentence.

Applications, Connections and Extensions

Every exercise in this book is designed to support you as you learn appropriate theories and apply them to problems. In the labs, you demonstrate your understanding of a theory only by applying the theory. In the quizzes and projects, you are invited to make further connections and extensions of your learning.

Table Manners
Student Exercises

The Bohr - Rutherford Model ...

Lab 1.1: The Bohr-Rutherford Model of the Atom

What's The Question?
We know that there are only 96 naturally occurring elements. Yet from them, millions of compounds can form. Each of the 96 elements is unique. In this experiment, you will heat atoms of elements in very hot flames, and observe their characteristic colors. Each of the 96 elements has its own set of colors.

What are atoms made of? What are they like inside? Whatever model we scientists think up to answer these questions must also explain everything else we know about matter.

What Are We Doing?

1. Your teacher will either set up Bunsen burners, or tell you how to safely light your own.

2. Choose a wooden splint that has been soaked in a compound. *Do not mix chemicals!!*

3. Hold the wooden splint in the Bunsen burner flame for a few seconds. Observe and record the color.

4. When the stick begins to burn, plunge it back into the proper container to wet it again.

5. Repeat with other chemicals, until you have tested all of the solutions.

What Are We Thinking About?

1. Name the positive particles in the atom.

2. Where are the positive particles found?

3. Where are the negative particles found in the atom? What are they called?

4. Describe the force between the electrons and the protons in the atom.

Questions For Later...

1. Do all compounds containing copper make the same colors? Explain your thinking.

2. You would like to test a small sample of soil to see if it contained strontium. What would you do with the soil? How would you know that it contained strontium?

3. Why do different elements have different colors in the flame? In your complete sentences, use the words *proton*, *electron*, *neutron*, and *energy level*.

© Ross Lattner Publishing   www.rosslattner.ca

... and the Spectrum of the Atom

Name:
Date:

Focus Question: Write the question that you are trying to answer.

1 **Experiment:** Test each of the solutions provided by your teacher. Carefully record the name of the metal in the compound, and the color of the flame.

2 **Explain using pictures and sentences:** Why does each atom have its own unique color?

#	Metal	Description of Color
1		
2		
3		
4		
5		
6		
7		
8		
9		
10		
11		
12		

3 **Refine your Explanation** using diagrams and sentences.

© Ross Lattner Publishing   www.rosslattner.ca

Organization of the Periodic Table

Name:
Date:

Activity 1.2: Organization of the Periodic Table

Look up the term *periodic table* or *periodic table of the elements* in the index of your text book or another reference. Use your text to complete the periodic table on the opposite page.

1. In each rectangle, print neatly all of the following information: *Name, Symbol (X), Atomic Number (Z), Mass Number (A)*.

2. Label each column 1, 2, 3, ... 18 etc, according to the table in your text book.

3. Obtain three colored markers, or highlighters. Highlight all of the *non-metals* one Color, the *metals* another Color, and the borderline cases, the *metalloids*, a third Color. What pattern do you notice?

4. A large group of elements are called the *transition metals*. Where are they on the periodic table? Look them up in your text book, in an encyclopedia, or the Internet.

5. Label the *alkali metal* group or family of elements.

6. Label the *alkali earth metals* group or family of elements.

7. Label the *halogens* and the *noble gases*.

N⁷	Xᶻ
Nitrogen	Name
14.01	A

The Bohr-Rutherford Periodic Table

Name:
Date:

Activity 1.3: Bohr, Rutherford and the Periodic Table

What's The Question?

The Bohr-Rutherford model tells us a great deal about the structure of individual atoms. *What is the relationship between the Bohr-Rutherford model of the atom, and the structure of the periodic table?*

Electrons
All of the Electrons
All of the Negative Charge
0.05% of the mass

What Are We Doing?

1. Fill in the electrons as shown in the example. The first two electrons go to the innermost level, close to the attractive positive nucleus. Remaining electrons go into the next closest level until it is filled.

2. Print the number of protons (+) and neutrons (n) inside the nucleus.

3. Print the symbol and the name for the element.

4. Label the Group at the top of each column (1, 2, 13, 14...etc.).

5. Label the Row at the left of each period (1, 2, 3 etc).

What Are We Thinking About?

- The electrons carry all of the negative charge, and a very tiny amount of mass. They fly about at very great speed some distance from the nucleus. Because of their negative charge, they are attracted to the positive nucleus.

- The nucleus is very tiny. If the atom is as big as the larger circle, the nucleus is about $\frac{1}{10\,000}$ the size shown in the diagram. Despite its tiny size, the nucleus contains all of the positive charge, and nearly all of the mass of the atom.

- Protons and neutrons inside the nucleus have almost the same mass: about 1.00 atomic mass units. Protons carry one positive charge, while neutrons carry no charge. Electrons carry one negative charge, and have a mass of $\frac{1}{2\,000}$ atomic mass units.

Nucleus
All of the Protons
All of the Neutrons
All of the Positive Charge
99.95% of the mass

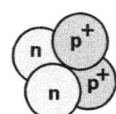

Questions For Later ... Answer all of these on a separate page.

1. What is the same about the electron arrangement of every element in a column (group)? What is different?

2. What is the same about the electron arrangement of every element in a row (period)? What is different?

14   Si

The Table of Atomic Cores

Name:
Date:

Activity 1.4: Valence Electrons, Atomic Cores and the Periodic Table

What's The Question? The Bohr-Rutherford model of the atom has a lot of parts. *Can we simplify the model to make it easier to use?*

What Are We Thinking About?
Chemists have found that only the electrons in the outermost, partially filled shell directly affect the chemistry of the atom. These outermost electrons are called the *valence electrons*. All of the other electrons in the inner, completely filled shells, are called *core electrons*. Like the seeds in the apple core, they are buried close to the center of the atom.

What Are We Doing?
For each element in the Bohr-Rutherford periodic table, perform the following steps, and write your results on the Core Valence table below.

1. Draw a light dotted line between the *valence* electrons and the *core* electrons as shown in the example. The valence electrons are in the outermost, partially filled shell. The core electrons are in the inner, completely filled shells.

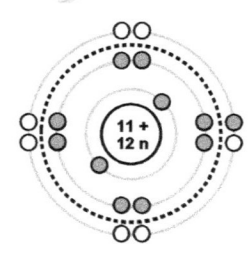

2. Add up all of the charges in the *atomic core*. In this case, there are 10 core electrons plus 11 protons. The total charge on the atomic core is positive one (+1).

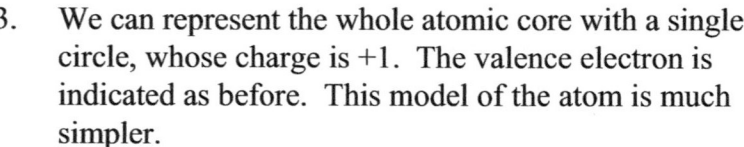

3. We can represent the whole atomic core with a single circle, whose charge is +1. The valence electron is indicated as before. This model of the atom is much simpler.

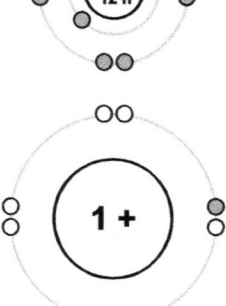

3. Complete the core - valence diagrams for each element. Print the symbol and name for the element.

4. Label the Group at the top of each column (1, 2, 13, 14...etc.)

5. Label the Row at the left of each period (1, 2, 3 etc).

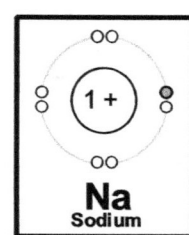

Questions For Later ....
1. What is the relationship between group number, and the number of valence electrons?

2. What is the relationship between group number, and the charge on the atomic core?

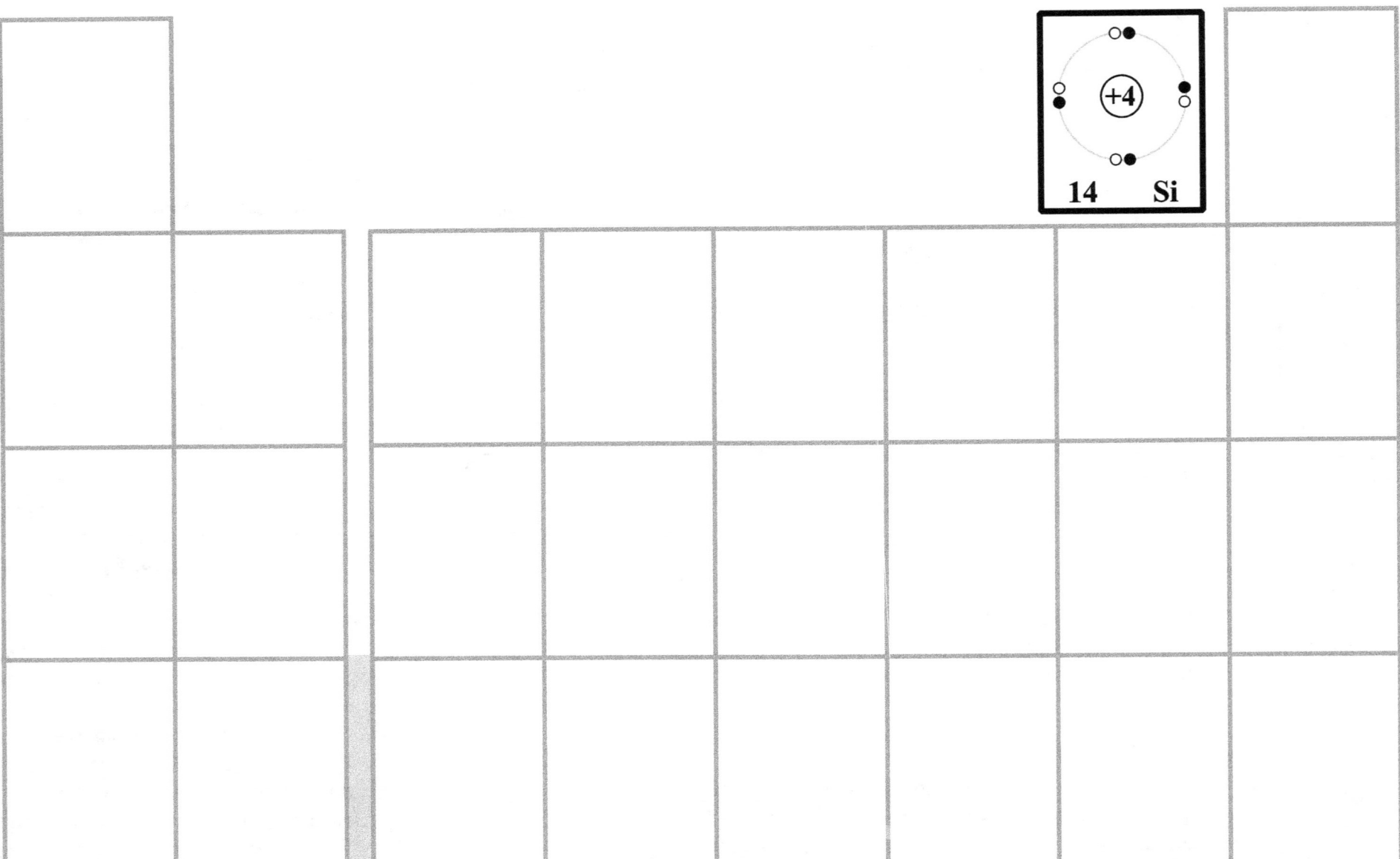

The Ross Periodic Table

Name:
Date:

Activity 1.5: Atomic Radius and the Periodic Table

What's The Question? How does the changing atomic core charge affect the size of the atom?

What Are We Doing?
1. Plot the radii from the table onto the graph.
2. Color the metals blue, the non-metals red.

Atomic Number	Element Symbol	Atomic Radius	Atomic Number	Element Symbol	Atomic Radius
1	H	0.032	11	Na	0.186
2	He	0.031	12	Mg	0.136
3	Li	0.152	13	Al	0.118
4	Be	0.089	14	Si	0.111
5	B	0.082	15	P	0.106
6	C	0.077	16	S	0.102
7	N	0.075	17	Cl	0.099
8	O	0.073	18	Ar	0.098
9	F	0.072	19	K	0.227
10	Ne	0.071	20	Ca	0.174

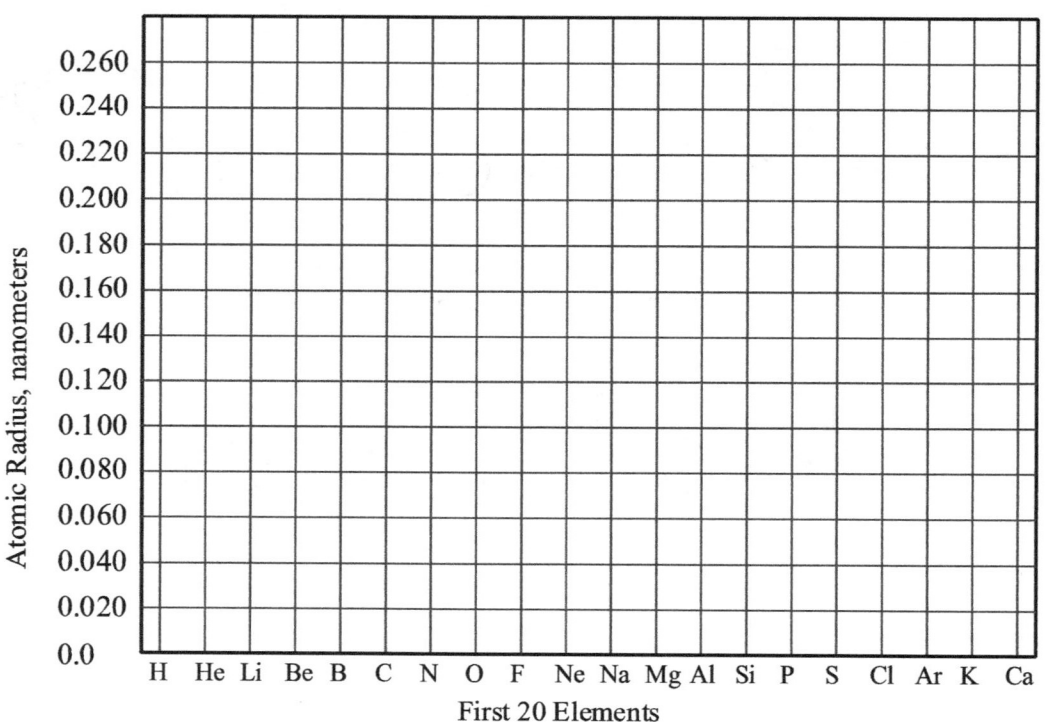

In the periodic table below:
1. complete each box by drawing in the valence electrons, printing the atomic core charge, and the name, number and symbol of the element.
2. Color the atomic cores of the metals blue, non-metals red, and metalloids yellow.

Questions For Later...
1. Describe how the atomic radius changes as you read from left to right across a row. Why does this happen?

2. Describe the change in atomic radius as you read down each family. Explain why this happens.

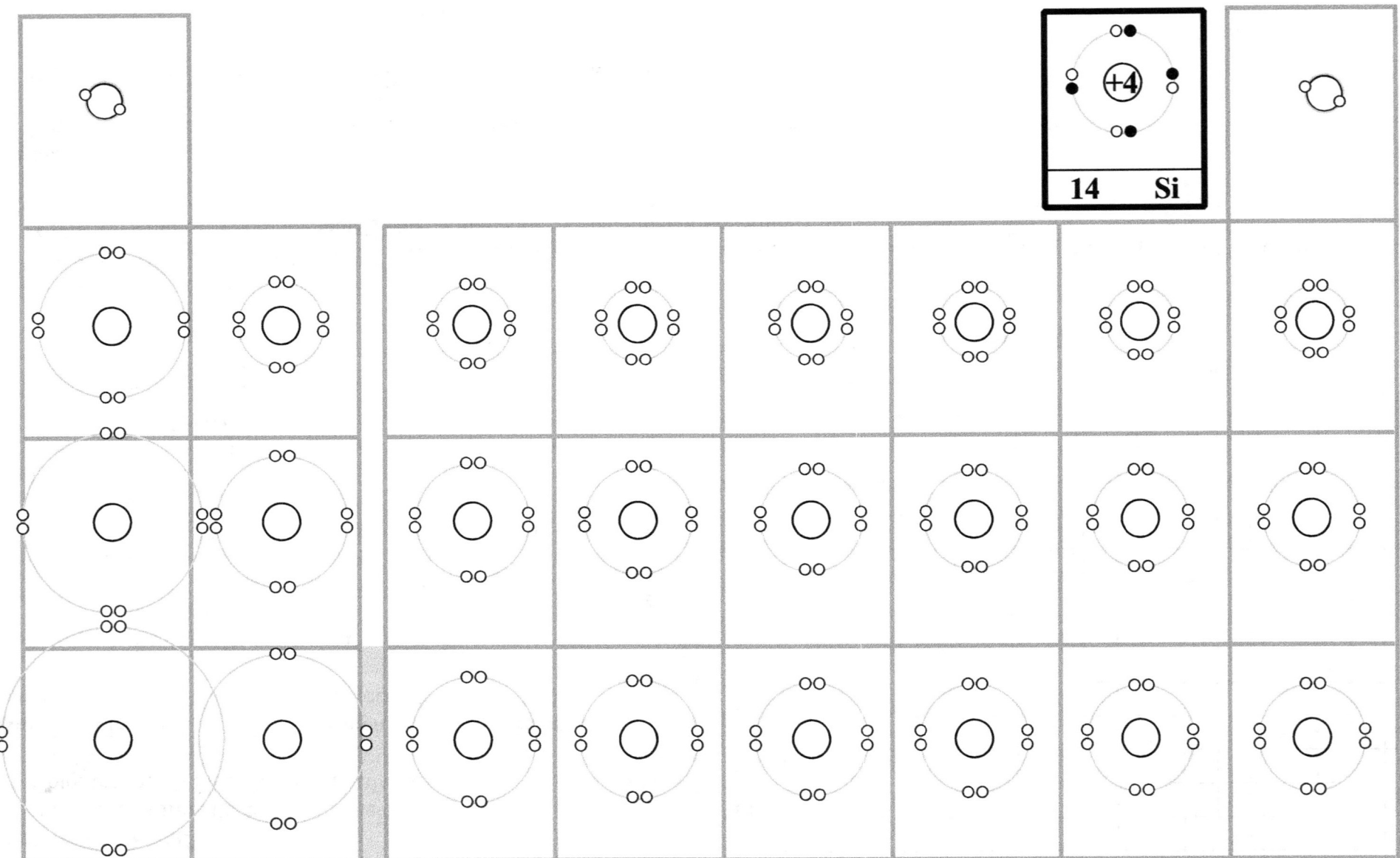

Resource 1.6: The Standard Periodic Table

1																	18
1 2.1 **H** Hydrogen 1.01	2											13	14	15	16	17	**2** — **He** Helium 4.00
3 1.0 **Li** Lithium 6.9	**4** 1.5 **Be** Beryllium 9.01											**5** 2.0 **B** Boron 10.8	**6** 2.5 **C** Carbon 12.01	**7** 3.0 **N** Nitrogen 14.01	**8** 3.5 **O** Oxygen 16.00	**9** 4.0 **F** Fluorine 19.0	**10** — **Ne** Neon 20.2
11 0.9 **Na** Sodium 23.0	**12** 1.2 **Mg** Magnesium 24.3	3	4	5	6	7	8	9	10	11	12	**13** 1.5 **Al** Aluminum 27.0	**14** 1.8 **Si** Silicon 28.1	**15** 2.1 **P** Phosphorus 31.0	**16** 2.5 **S** Sulfur 32.1	**17** 3.0 **Cl** Chlorine 35.5	**18** — **Ar** Argon 39.9
19 0.8 **K** Potassium 39.1	**20** 1.0 **Ca** Calcium 40.1	**21** 1.3 **Sc** Scandium 45.0	**22** 1.5 **Ti** Titanium 47.9	**23** 1.6 **V** Vanadium 50.9	**24** 1.6 **Cr** Chromium 52.0	**25** 1.5 **Mn** Manganese 54.9	**26** 1.8 **Fe** Iron 55.8	**27** 1.8 **Co** Cobalt 58.9	**28** 1.8 **Ni** Nickel 58.7	**29** 1.9 **Cu** Copper 63.5	**30** 1.6 **Zn** Zinc 65.4	**31** 1.6 **Ga** Gallium 69.7	**32** 1.8 **Ge** Germanium 72.6	**33** 2.0 **As** Arsenic 74.9	**34** 2.4 **Se** Selenium 79.0	**35** 2.8 **Br** Bromine 79.9	**36** — **Kr** Krypton 83.8
37 0.8 **Rb** Rubidium 85.5	**38** 1.0 **Sr** Strontium 87.6	**39** 1.2 **Y** Yttrium 88.9	**40** 1.4 **Zr** Zirconium 91.2	**41** 1.6 **Nb** Niobium 92.9	**42** 1.8 **Mo** Molybdenum 95.9	**43** 1.9 **Tc** Technicium (98)	**44** 2.2 **Ru** Ruthenium 101.1	**45** 2.2 **Rh** Rhodium 102.9	**46** 2.2 **Pd** Palladium 106.4	**47** 1.9 **Ag** Silver 107.9	**48** 1.7 **Cd** Cadmium 112.4	**49** 1.7 **In** Indium 114.8	**50** 1.8 **Sn** Tin 118.7	**51** 1.8 **Sb** Antimony 121.8	**52** 2.1 **Te** Tellurium 127.6	**53** 2.5 **I** Iodine 126.9	**54** — **Xe** Xenon 131.3
55 0.7 **Cs** Cesium 133	**56** 0.9 **Ba** Barium 137.3	**71** 1.2 **Lu** Lutetium 175	**72** 1.3 **Hf** Hafnium 178.5	**73** 1.5 **Ta** Tantalum 180.9	**74** 1.7 **W** Tungsten 183.8	**75** 1.9 **Re** Rhenium 186.2	**76** 2.2 **Os** Osmium 190.2	**77** 2.2 **Ir** Iridium 192.2	**78** 2.2 **Pt** Platinum 195.1	**79** 2.4 **Au** Gold 197.0	**80** 1.9 **Hg** Mercury 200.6	**81** 1.8 **Tl** Thallium 204.4	**82** 1.8 **Pb** Lead 207.2	**83** 1.9 **Bi** Bismuth 209.0	**84** 2.0 **Po** Polonium (209)	**85** 2.2 **At** Astatine (210)	**86** — **Rn** Radon (222)
87 0.7 **Fr** Francium (223)	**88** 0.9 **Ra** Radium (226)	**103** **Lr** Lawrencium (256)	**104** **Unc**	**105** **Unp**	**106** **Unh**	**107** **Uns**	**108** **Uno**	**109** **Une**									

Lanthanide Series

57 1.1 **La** Lanthanum 138.9	**58** 1.1 **Ce** Cerium 140.1	**59** 1.1 **Pr** Praseodymium 140.9	**60** 1.1 **Nd** Neodymium 144.2	**61** 1.1 **Pm** Promethium (145)	**62** 1.1 **Sm** Samarium 150.4	**63** 1.1 **Eu** Europium 150.2	**64** 1.1 **Gd** Gadolinium 157.2	**65** 1.1 **Tb** Terbium 158.9	**66** 1.1 **Dy** Dysprosium 162.5	**67** 1.1 **Ho** Holmium 162.5	**68** 1.1 **Er** Erbium 167.3	**69** 1.1 **Tm** Thulium 168.9	**70** 1.1 **Yb** Ytterbium 173.0

Actinide Series

89 1.1 **Ac** Actinium (227)	**90** 1.1 **Th** Thorium 232.0	**91** 1.5 **Pa** Protactinium (231)	**92** 1.7 **U** Uranium 238.0	**93** 1.3 **Np** Neptunium (237)	**94** 1.3 **Pu** Plutonium (244)	**95** 1.3 **Am** Americium (243)	**96** 1.3 **Cm** Curium (247)	**97** 1.3 **Bk** Berkelium (247)	**98** 1.3 **Cf** Californium (251)	**99** 1.3 **Es** Einsteinium (254)	**100** 1.3 **Fm** Fermium (253)	**101** 1.3 **Md** Mendelevium (257)	**102** 1.3 **No** Nobelium (255)

Key box: Atomic Number, Electronegativity, Symbol, Name, Mass

This version of the periodic table includes all of the elements. We shall be concerned primarily with the elements indicated in the white boxes. The others are complicated enough that they still surprise professional chemists. To understand them, you will have to learn more elaborate theories in your next chemistry course.

You can say something nice, dear, if you think long enough

How Good are your Table Manners?

Quiz 1: The Ross Periodic Table

Some of the words needed for this page can be found in the list at the bottom of the page.

1. Complete the Bohr-Rutherford diagram below for the atom aluminum-27. $^{27}_{13}Al$

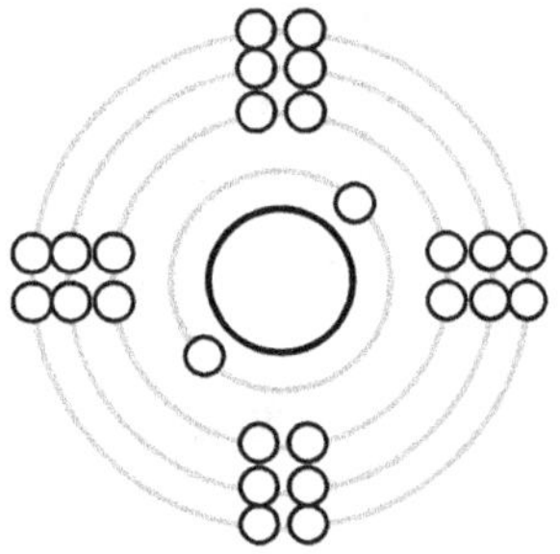

   _____ heavy particles in the nucleus
   _____ Number of protons
   _____ Number of neutrons
   _____ Number of electrons

   Number of

   Date: _____   / 5

2. Complete the Bohr-Rutherford diagram below for the atom oxygen-16. $^{16}_{8}O$

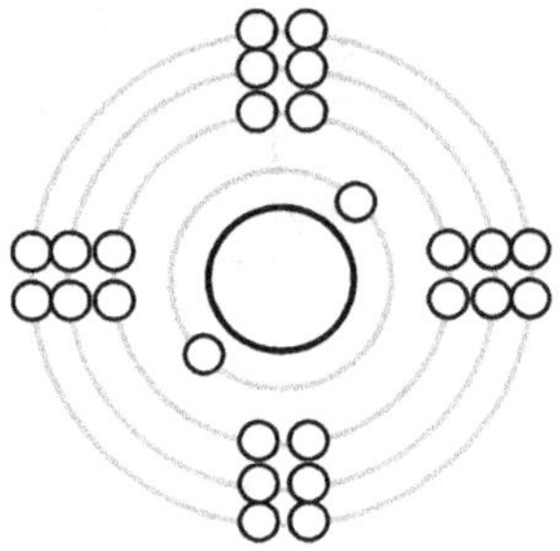

   _____ heavy particles in the nucleus
   _____ Number of protons
   _____ Number of neutrons
   _____ Number of electrons

   Number of

   Date: _____   / 5

3. Which *family* or *group* of elements is indicated by each letter?

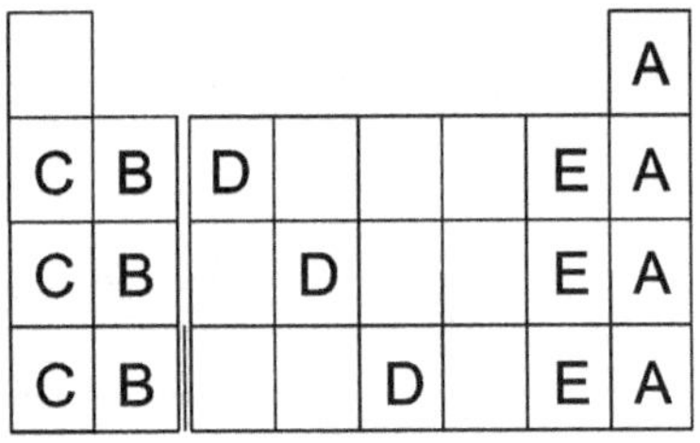

   A _____   D _____

   B _____   E _____

   C _____

   Date: _____   / 5

4. How many electrons are present in the valence shell for each of the indicated atoms?

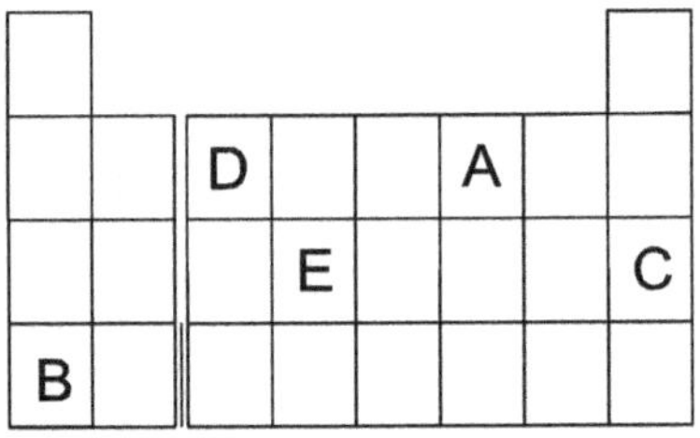

   A _____   D _____

   B _____   E _____

   C _____

   Date: _____   / 5

Metal	Alkali metal	Noble Gas	Electron
Non-metal	Alkali earth metal	Proton	Heavy Particle
Metalloid	Halogen	Neutron	Shell

© Ross Lattner Publishing   48   www.rosslattner.ca

You can say something nice, dear, if you think long enough
How Good are your Table Manners?

Quiz 1:   The Ross Periodic Table   Name:

---

5   Complete the Bohr-Rutherford diagram below for the atom potassium-39. $^{39}_{19}K$

_____ Number of heavy particles in the nucleus

_____ Number of protons

_____ Number of neutrons

_____ Number of electrons

Date: / 5

---

6   Complete the Bohr-Rutherford diagram below for the atom calcium-40. $^{40}_{20}Ca$

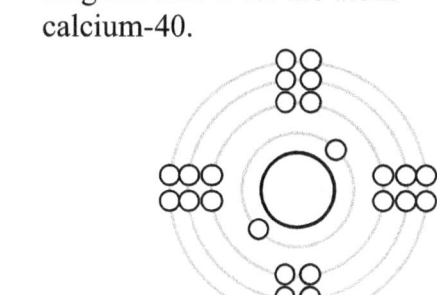

_____ Number of heavy particles in the nucleus

_____ Number of protons

_____ Number of neutrons

_____ Number of electrons

Date: / 5

7

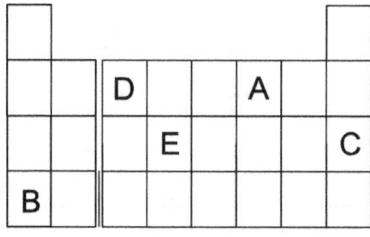

Mark one box in the table with each letter:

A   same row, smaller than A
B   one more valence electron than B
C   same group as C, but smaller
D   same row as D, but more like a metal
E   same group as E, but larger

Date: / 5

8

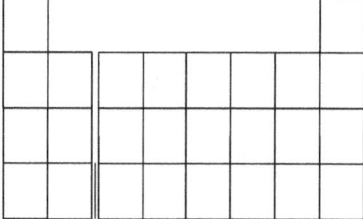

Mark all of the boxes with the appropriate letters to indicate:

A   all of the Noble Gases
B   all of the Alkali Metals
C   all of the Halogens
D   all of the Metalloids
E   all of the Alkali Earth metals

Date: / 5

You can say something nice, dear, if you think long enough

How Good are your Table Manners?

Quiz 1: The Ross Periodic Table Name:

9 Complete the valence-core diagram below for the element sulfur. $^{32}_{16}S$

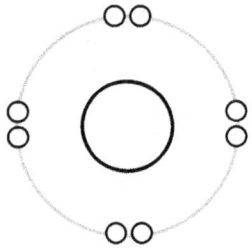

_____ positive charges in the atomic core
_____ number of valence electrons

Date: / 5

10 Complete the valence-core diagram below for the element carbon. $^{12}_{6}C$

_____ positive charges in the atomic core
_____ number of valence electrons

Date: / 5

11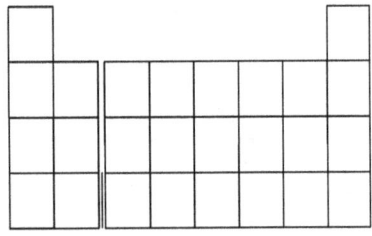

Mark boxes A , B , C etc. to indicate:

A the element with only one electron
B the smallest Noble gas
C most likely to grab and hold an extra electron
D group 1 element most likely to lose an electron
E group 5 element most likely to grab and hold an extra electron

Date: / 5

12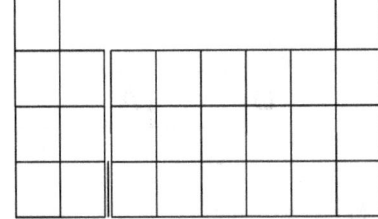

Mark boxes A , B , C etc. to indicate:

A a halogen smaller than chlorine
B group 6 element bigger than sulfur
C row 3 metal whose electrons are more loosely held than those of magnesium
D group 1 element that is not a metal
E row 3 element with a full valence shell

Date: / 5

© Ross Lattner Publishing   50   www.rosslattner.ca

Table Manners
Student Exercises

Movement of Electrons

Activity 2.1: If you were an electron... where would you go?

What's The Question? We have studied the core charge, the valence electrons and the radius of the elements of the short table.

When we compare any two elements of the periodic table, which element has the greater ability to attract and hold one more valence electron?

What Are We Doing? Each box on the opposite page has two atoms, and one free electron. The electron is free to move to either atom.

1. **Predict** which of the two atoms will the electron tend to move toward? Draw an arrow to show the movement.

2. **Explain** your prediction in words.

3. **Check** your predictions with the teacher. Make corrections.

4. For any errors, **explain** how your thinking has changed.

What Are We Thinking About?

- The larger an atom's core charge, the greater its ability to attract and hold one more valence electron.

- The smaller an atom's radius, the greater its ability to attract and hold one more valence electron.

- A free electron can only move into a vacant space in a valence shell.

Question: would the electron move to O, or to Mg?

Predict: the free electron will tend to move into the vacant space in the Oxygen valence.

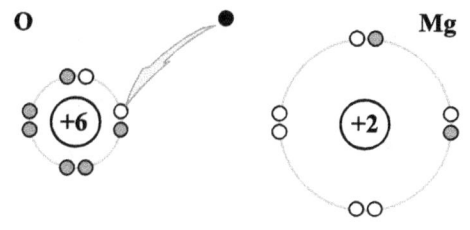

Explain: Oxygen has both a greater core charge and a smaller radius than magnesium. Electrons tend to move as close as possible to the greatest core charge. Our electron will move into a vacant space in oxygen's valence shell, as close as possible to the +6 core charge.

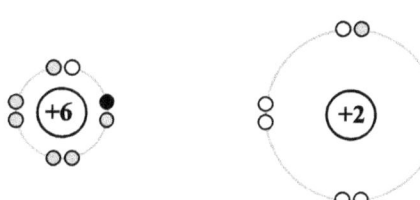

Questions For Later...

1. Elements in Group 18 are called "noble gases" They have a core charge of +8 and very small radii. Why do these atoms *not* attract and hold additional electrons?

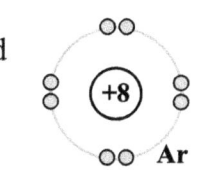

2. Of the eight questions on the opposite page, which *two* questions did you find the most difficult to answer? Why were they difficult?

Elements of the Ross Table

Name:
Date:

Focus Question: Each box contains two atoms and a free electron. Toward which atom will the electron tend to move? **Predict** with an arrow, **draw** the electron, and **explain** using words.

1 Ca • F 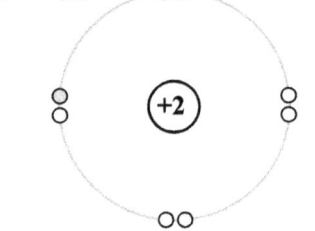	*2* F • Br 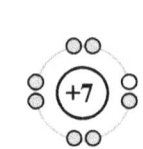 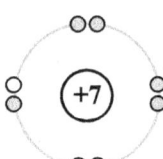
3 O Ne 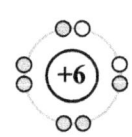 • 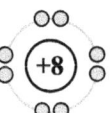	*4* H • Na 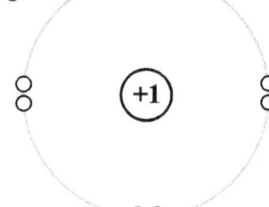
5 Ge • Al 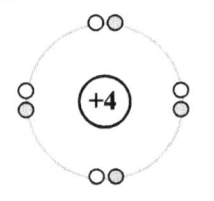 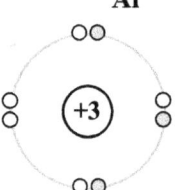	*6* S • H 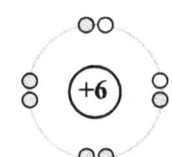
7 H F • 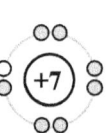	*8* C • P 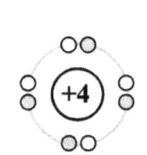 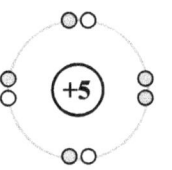

© Ross Lattner Publishing   www.rosslattner.ca

Table Manners
Student Exercises

Electronegativity χ

Activity 2.2: Electronegativity

What's The Question? Scientists define *electronegativity* as "a measure of the relative tendency of an atom to attract electrons to itself when chemically combined with another atom." The symbol for electronegativity is the Greek letter *chi*, or χ

How is electronegativity related to the core charge, valence electrons and radius of the atoms on the periodic table?

What Are We Thinking About? Electronegativity χ is a number between 0.7 and 4.0.

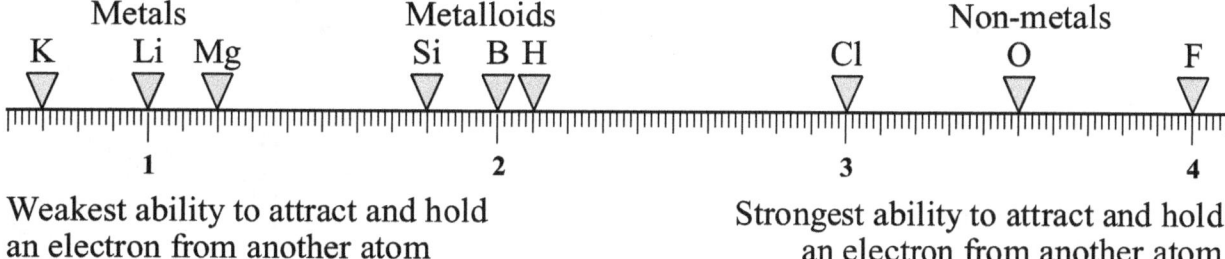

Weakest ability to attract and hold an electron from another atom

Strongest ability to attract and hold an electron from another atom

What Are We Doing?

1. The Ross table on the opposite page contains the electronegativities for all of the elements on the table. Complete the table by adding the core charge, valence electrons, name, symbol and number.

2. On page 51, you had predicted whether a free electron would tend to move toward one atom or the other. (the black electron indicated by the grey arrow on Fluorine in the diagram at right).

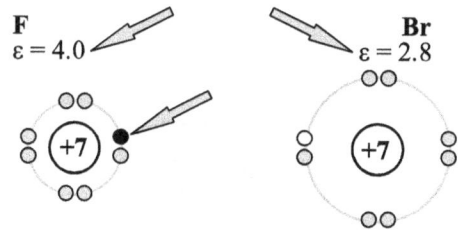

3. On your answers on page 51, write the values for χ near the symbols for each atom. (See the grey arrows in the diagram above right).

4. A free electron would always tend to move toward the atom with the greatest electronegativity. Use the electronegativities to check *all* of your predictions on page 51.

5. Were your initial predictions on page 51 correct? If not, in what way did you have to change your thinking?

Elements of the Ross Table

Name:
Date:

In addition to the Ross diagram, each cell of the periodic table below contains the value of χ.
Complete this table by adding:

    a) the core charges
    b) the valence electrons
    c) the atomic number and symbol, as shown.

Example cell shown: 1.5, +3, 13 Al

Questions For Later...

1. The core charges of the atoms tend to increase as you read across any row of the periodic table. What effect does that appear to have on electronegativity? Explain your answer.

2. The radius of the atoms tends to increase as you read down any column of the periodic table. What effect does that appear to have on electronegativity? Explain.

3. In the last column of the periodic table, all of the elements have full valence shells. What effect does that have on electronegativity? (Hint: review the definition of electronegativity before you answer.)

© Ross Lattner Publishing   www.rosslattner.ca

Table Manners
Student Exercises

The Metals

Activity 2.3: The Metals

What's The Question? The periodic table at right contains metals and non-metals. Quick: from memory alone, use a pencil to mark the metals **M** .

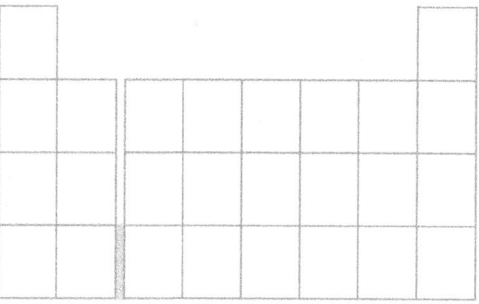

Check answers with a text. Make corrections if needed.

What is it that makes metals metallic? What is it that makes non-metals behave the way that they do?

What Tests Are We Using?

- **Electrical Conductivity:** apply leads of a conductivity tester.   *Conductor / Non-conductor.*
- **Thermal Conductivity:** Hold against an ice cube. Can you feel   *Conductor / Non-conductor.*
  heat leaving your finger?
- **Reflectivity:** Does the element look silvery or dull?   *Reflective / Dull.*
- **Malleability:** tap the sample lightly with a retort rod or spoon.   *Dents / Shatters.*

What Are We Doing? You will be given samples of two metals: aluminum and magnesium.

1. **Identify** the two elements, and write a brief description of each element's appearance.
2. **Draw** a scale Ross diagram of each element. Size is important! Include *core charge*, *valence electrons* and *electronegativity*.
3. **Test** each element, using the tests indicated above.

What Are We Thinking About? A Metal like lithium has a small atomic core charge, and a large radius. Its valence electrons are very far from the weak core charge, and are therefore easy to remove.

Because the electrons are easy to move, they tend to "float" from atom to atom. Easily moved electrons carry electrical current, and allow heat energy to flow through a metal. Use your pencil to trace the movement of one of the electrons as it "floats" from the valence of one atom to the another.

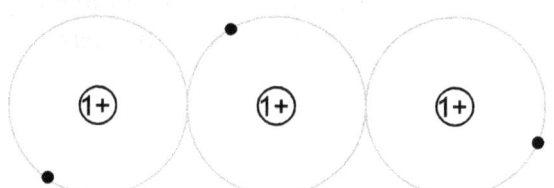

In the same way, when we heat a metal, we make all parts of the atoms move more quickly, including the electrons. A "hot" or rapidly moving electron can move to a different part of the metal, conducting its heat energy quickly from one part of the metal to another.

Light interacts with matter by making electrons move. The electrons in the metal are free to move. When light strikes a metal, the electrons can respond by vibrating quickly in response to the light. Their rapid motion causes the ray of light to "bounce" off the surface, obeying the law of reflection.

Finally, each atom in a metal is held in place by the sea of electrons that move easily from atom to atom. When we hit a metal with a hammer, the atoms can just slide around in this loose sea of electrons. Thus, metals tend to bend or to dent rather than to shatter.

Elements of the Ross Table

Name:
Date:

Element Name & Description	Draw scale Ross diagram	Test	Observable Properties
Magnesium:	(+2 with 1.2 shell, 2 electrons on each side)	Electrical Conductivity Thermal Conductivity Reflectivity Malleability Metal or non-metal?	
Aluminum		Electrical Conductivity Thermal Conductivity Reflectivity Malleability Metal or non-metal?	

Questions For Later...

1. You find an element that has a small core charge and a large radius. Will that element be a metal or a non-metal? Explain.

2. Copper is clearly a metal. Imagine that you were to test copper in the same way as in this lab. Predict the results for copper.

3. List the names of ten to twenty metals from the periodic table on page 51. Find the electronegativity of each metal. How many of them have electronegativity χ greater than 2.0?

4. Describe the core charge, the radius and the number of valence electrons you would expect for a typical metal.

5. Almost all metals have electronegativity less than 2.0. Explain why this is the case, using your answer to (4) above.

Table Manners
Student Exercises

The Non-Metals

Activity 2.4: The Non-Metals

What's The Question? The periodic table at right contains 26 elements, 14 of which are non-metals. From memory alone, use a pencil to mark the non-metals **N**.

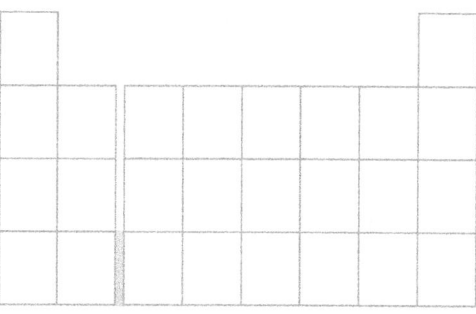

Check answers with a text. Make corrections if needed.

What is it that makes non-metals behave the way that they do?

What Tests Are We Using?

- **Electrical Conductivity:** apply leads of a conductivity tester. *Conductor / Non-conductor.*
- **Thermal Conductivity:** Hold against an ice cube. Can you feel heat leaving your finger? *Conductor / Non-conductor.*
- **Reflectivity:** Does the element look silvery or dull? *Reflective / Dull.*
- **Malleability:** tap the sample lightly with a retort rod or spoon. *Dents / Shatters.*

What Are We Doing? You will be given samples of two non-metals: carbon and sulfur.

1. **Identify** the two elements, and write a brief description of each element's appearance.
2. **Draw** a scale Ross diagram of each element. Size is important! Include *core charge, valence electrons* and *electronegativity*.
3. **Test** each element, using the tests indicated above.

What are we thinking about? A Non-Metal like fluorine has a large core charge, and a small radius. It holds its electrons very tightly. Fluorine is very small and has a strong core charge. Not only does it hold on to its own electrons, it is even able to attract electrons away from other atoms, and keep them in its own valence.

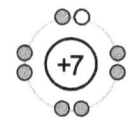

All Non metals hold their electrons very tightly. Since the electrons cannot move very far, they can carry neither electric current (flow of electrons) nor the thermal energy of electrons. Non-metals are almost always poor conductors of heat and electricity.

Because light cannot make the electrons move freely in non-metals, most non-metals are clear or colored or opaque, but not shiny. Think of carbon, sulfur, oxygen, or chlorine.

Apart from that, their variety is amazing. Non-metals can be solids, liquids, or gases. Non-metals are not as tough as metals in most cases. They can be either brittle or flexible. If a solid non-metal is hit by a hammer, it tends to shatter into pieces. Sometimes solid non-metals behave like wax or plastic.

© Ross Lattner Publishing   www.rosslattner.ca

Elements of the Ross Table

Name:
Date:

Element Name & Description	Draw scale Ross diagram	Test	Observable Properties
Carbon: a black, crumbly solid that...	2.5 (+4 diagram)	Electrical Conductivity	
		Thermal Conductivity	
		Reflectivity	
		Malleability	
		Metal or non-metal?	
		Electrical Conductivity	
		Thermal Conductivity	
		Reflectivity	
		Malleability	
		Metal or non-metal?	

Questions For Later...

1. You find an element that has a large core charge and a small radius. Will that element be a metal or a non-metal? Explain.

2. Iodine is a non-metal. Imagine that you were to test copper and iodine in the same way as in this lab. Predict the results for copper and iodine.

3. Non-metals have a large core charge and a small radius. How do these things give a non metal its observable properties?

4. Use the periodic table on page 51 to find the electronegativities of all 14 non metals you identified at the beginning of this exercise. What is the lowest electronegativity that you can find?

5. All of the non-metals have electronegativity greater than 2.0. Explain why this is the case, using the words *core*, *valence* and *radius* in your sentences as you answer.

© Ross Lattner Publishing   www.rosslattner.ca

Table Manners
Student Exercises

the Metalloids

Activity 2.5: The Metalloids

What's The Question? The metalloids is a class of elements that have some of the properties of metals, and some of the properties of non-metals. They lie on the dividing line between the metals and non-metals. Use a pencil to mark the metall**o**ids **O**. Check your answers with a text. Make corrections if needed.

What are the metalloids? What is it that makes metalloids behave as they do?

What Are We Doing? You will be given samples of three elements: aluminum, carbon and silicon.

1. **Identify** the three elements, and write a brief description of each element's appearance.
2. **Draw** a scale Ross diagram of each element. Size is important! Include *core charge*, *valence electrons* and *electronegativity*.
3. **Test** the silicon, or observe your teacher testing it. You already have the results for Al and C.

Element Name & Description	Draw scale Ross diagram	Test	Observable Properties
Silicon:		Electrical Conductivity	
		Thermal Conductivity	
		Reflectivity	
		Malleability	
		Metal or non-metal?	
Aluminum		Electrical Conductivity	
		Thermal Conductivity	
		Reflectivity	
		Malleability	
		Metal or non-metal?	
Carbon		Electrical Conductivity	
		Thermal Conductivity	
		Reflectivity	
		Malleability	
		Metal or non-metal?	

Elements of the Ross Table

Name:
Date:

Questions For Later...

1. Complete the Ross diagram at right, and use a colored marker to indicate the metalloids boron, silicon and arsenic. (Note: germanium is also considered a metalloid, but it is more metallic than silicon.)

2. List the electronegativity χ for the three metalloids.
   a) What is the approximate value of electronegativity for a metalloid?

   b) What effect does increasing core charge have upon electronegativity?

   c) What effect does increasing radius have upon electronegativity?

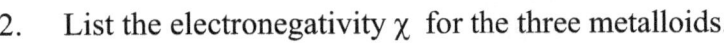

Let's go on a walk through the elements. Start with your pencil on boron. Travel south to aluminum, then turn east to silicon and phosphorus. Finally, turn south again and end the trip at arsenic. Repeat the journey back and forth several times, until you are familiar with it.

3. On the first leg of the journey, you went from B to Al. You traveled from a metalloid to a metal.

   a) List the differences and similarities in Ross (core, valence and radius) between the two elements.

   b) Use your answer to (a) to explain why boron is a metalloid and aluminum is a metal.

4. On the second leg of the journey, we traveled from Al to Si, that is, from a metal to a metalloid. What similarities and differences in Ross could account for the change from metal to metalloid?

5. What similarities and differences in Ross could account for the shift from metalloid to non-metal behavior as you traveled from Si to P ?

6. What similarities and differences in Ross could account for the shift from non-metal to metalloid behavior as you traveled from P to As ?

© Ross Lattner Publishing   www.rosslattner.ca

Table Manners
Student Exercises
The Noble Gases

Activity 2.6: The Noble Gases

What's The Question? The "Noble" Gases were given that name as a little joke. These gases did not react. They did not "associate with the common elements," or form compounds with them. Use a pencil to mark the noble gases **G** in the periodic table at right. Check your answers with a text. Make corrections if needed.

What are the noble gases? What is it that makes noble gases behave as they do?

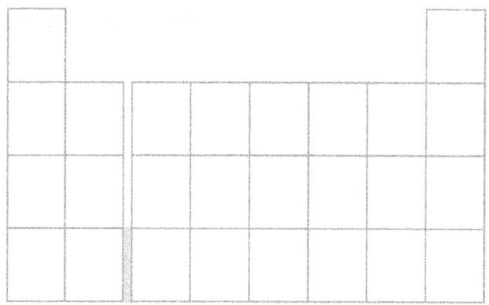

Questions For Later...

1. Complete the Ross table at right for the noble gases.

2. List the similarities and differences in the Ross diagrams of the noble gases.

3. The atomic cores of noble gases are all +8 (the exception being helium). How strongly would you expect a noble gas to hold on to its own valence electrons? Explain.

4. The noble gases have a very large core charge, with a very strong attraction for electrons. However, the noble gases do not grab and hold electrons from other atoms. Why not?

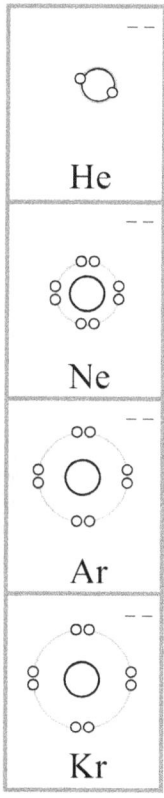

5. Helium is a curiosity. It only has a core charge of +2, like the metals magnesium and calcium. But far from behaving as a metal, helium is the least reactive of the noble gases. Why is that?

© Ross Lattner Publishing   www.rosslattner.ca

You can say something nice, dear, if you think long enough

How Good are your Table Manners?

Quiz 2: Elements of the Periodic Table

1. Given Magnesium and Fluorine...
Predict: toward which atom will the free electron tend to move?

   Mg   •   F

   Explain your prediction.

   Date: _____ / 5

2. List the elements in order, from least to greatest electronegativity.

   ____ ____ ____ ____ ____
   least   greatest

   Date: _____ / 5

3. Here is the second row of the periodic table. Complete the row by adding the *group number*, the *core charge* and *valence electrons*.

   Date: _____ / 5

4. Write the *name*, the *symbol* and the *electronegativity* χ of each element in Row 2 of the table.

   Date: _____ / 5   Date: _____ / 5

© Ross Lattner Publishing   www.rosslattner.ca

You can say something nice, dear, if you think long enough
How Good are your Table Manners?

Quiz 2: Elements of the Periodic Table   Name:

5   Two elements on the table have $\chi = 1.0$.

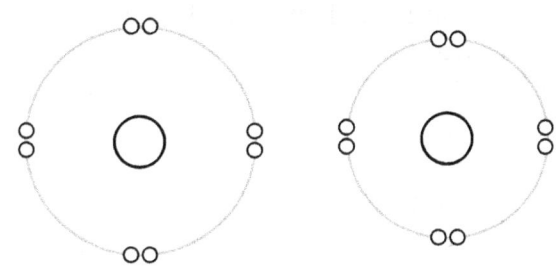

a)   Find the two elements, and name them.

b)   Complete the core valence radius diagrams.

c)   Are these metals, non-metals, metalloids or noble gases? Explain.

Date: _____   / 5

6   Given Chlorine and Bromine...
Predict: toward which atom will the free electron tend to move?

     Br   **Cl**

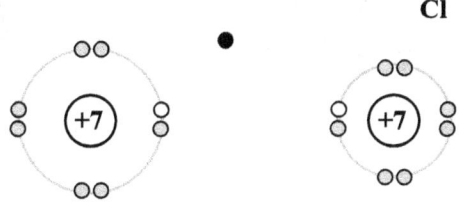

Explain your prediction.

Date: _____   / 5

7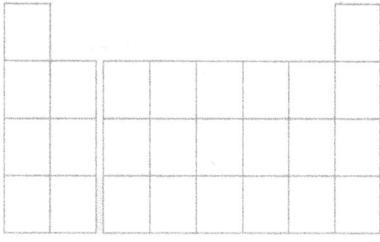

Mark boxes M, N, O etc. to indicate:

M   the metals

N   the non-metals

O   the metalloids

G   the noble gases

Date: _____   / 5

8   Two elements on the table have $\chi = 3.0$.

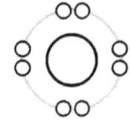 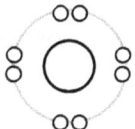

a)   Find the two elements, and name them.

b)   Complete the core valence radius diagrams.

c)   Are these metals, non-metals, metalloids or noble gases? Explain.

Date: _____   / 5

© Ross Lattner Publishing   www.rosslattner.ca

You can say something nice, dear, if you think long enough
How Good are your Table Manners?

Quiz 2: Elements of the Periodic Table   Name:

9 Two elements on the table have χ = 2.0. 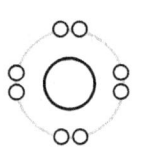 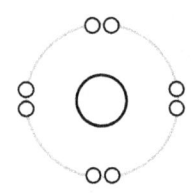 a) Find the two elements, and name them. b) Complete the core valence radius diagrams. c) Are these metals, non-metals, metalloids or noble gases? Explain. Date: / 5	10 Given Hydrogen and Sulfur... Predict: toward which atom will the free electron tend to move? S • H 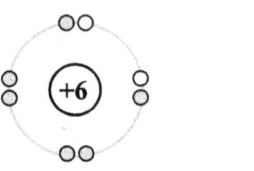 Explain your prediction. Date: / 5
11 Metals can be hammered and bent without breaking. They are shiny, good conductors of electricity and heat. Why is that? Explain, using Ross concepts. Date: / 5	12 Non-metals are poor conductors of heat and electricity. They are either clear or colored, never shiny. Why is that? Explain, using Ross concepts. Date: / 5

© Ross Lattner Publishing   www.rosslattner.ca

Table Manners
Student Exercises
Well Behaved Elements ...

Lab 3.1: Reactions of Group 17, the Halogens

Do you Remember? Complete the core - valence - radius diagrams below.

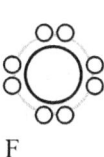 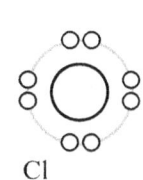 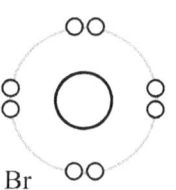 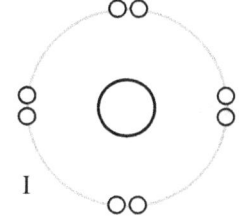

F   Cl   Br   I

What's The Question? The Group 17 elements are fluorine, chlorine, bromine and iodine. They are also called the *halogens*. In this lab, you will examine some of their properties.

Which halogens are most and least reactive?

What Are We Doing?

1. Label three clean strips of paper I, Br and Cl. Your teacher will place one drop each of a solution of iodine (I_2), bromine (Br_2) and chlorine (Cl_2) on the paper.

2. Gently waft some of the vapors toward your nose, and smell them. **Caution!** Describe the odor. Where else have you smelled things like that?

3. Photographs gradually fade over time. Will halogens cause a photo to fade? Your teacher will expose a photograph to Iodine and to Bromine, to see if they will cause the photo to fade.

4. *Predict* whether I_2 or Br_2 will be the strongest bleaching agent. *Explain* your prediction using core valence radius diagrams.

5. *Observe* how iodine and bromine react with the dyes in the photo.

6. *Explain* your observations, using Ross diagrams and sentences.

What Are We Thinking About?

Caution: Contact with Skin can cause chemical burns. Cl_2, Br_2 and I_2 are dangerous to touch or inhale. *Never take your goggles off during this lab. Even if you finish, others may still be working.*

- The halogens all have the same valence configuration and the same core charge. Which halogen attracts its electrons most strongly? Why?

- How many additional electrons can one halogen atom attract into its valence shell? Explain.

... of the Ross Periodic Table

Name:
Date:

Focus Question: Write the question that you are trying to answer.

1 **Predict:** Which halogen will be the most reactive bleaching agent... bromine, or iodine?	2 **Explain** your prediction, using both core - valence - radius diagrams, and sentences.
3 **Observe,** and record your observations here.	4 **Explain** your observations, using both core - valence - radius diagrams and sentences.

Questions For Later...

1. Which halogen is most able to react with colored dyes? Provide evidence for your claim.

2. Which halogen has the strongest attraction for electrons from other atoms? Explain.

3. Explain why halogens are the most reactive non-metals.

Table Manners
Student Exercises

Well Behaved Elements ...

Lab 3.2: Reactions of Group 1, the Alkali Metals

Do you Remember? Complete the core - valence - radius diagrams below.

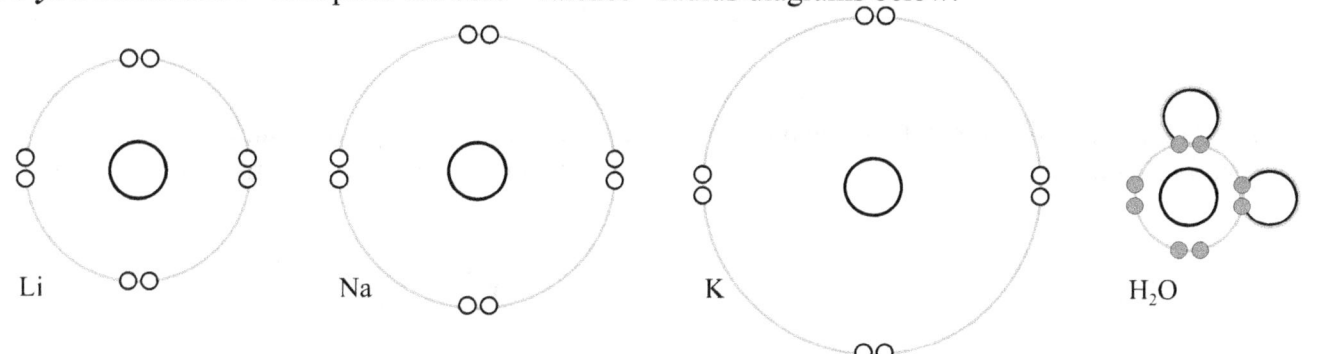

What's The Question? In the picture above, you can see which electrons are close to the +1 cores of the lithium, sodium and potassium atoms. You can also see the sizes and core charges of the hydrogen and oxygen atoms that make up water. Can water take an electron from an alkali metal? *From which alkali metal is the water most likely to take an electron?*

What Are We Doing?

Predict which metal is most reactive with water. *Explain* your prediction using diagrams like those above.

1. Put about 100 mL of fresh cold water in a 250 mL beaker. Dry the desk thoroughly.

2. Obtain a small (2 mm x 2 mm x 2 mm) piece of lithium in a petri dish. Cut it with a scoopula. Note its hardness, and the appearance of the fresh surface. Record.

3. Place the small piece of lithium in the water and immediately cover with the wire gauze. *Observe* from 1 m away. When the reaction ceases, record your observations.

4. Replace the water and repeat 2 – 3 with another metal.

5. Describe each element in your records. Use words that are easy to compare.

6. *Explain* your observations, using core - valence - radius diagrams and complete sentences.

What Are We Thinking About?

- **Caution: Danger of Fire, Caustic Products**. Li, Na and K are dangerous to touch, and react explosively with water. *Never take your goggles off during this lab: even if you finish, others may still be working.*

- All of the atoms have the same charge on their atomic cores, and the same number of valence electrons. Why would one metal be more reactive than another?

- What are the observable signs of a chemical change? Which visible signs are the most convincing to you?

© Ross Lattner Publishing   www.rosslattner.ca

... of the Ross Periodic Table

Name:
Date:

Focus Question: Write the question that you are trying to answer.

1	**Predict:** Which alkali metal will be most reactive with water?	2	**Explain** your prediction, using core - valence - radius diagrams and sentences.
3	**Observe** the hardness and activity of the alkali metals. Record your observations here.	4	**Explain** your observations, using core - valence - radius diagrams and sentences.

Questions For Later...

1. In Lab 3.1, the largest halogen atom was the least reactive. How do you explain the behavior of the alkali metals?

2. The alkali metal below potassium in the Group 1 elements is cesium. Would cesium be more or less reactive with water than potassium?

Table Manners
Student Exercises

Well Behaved Elements ...

Lab 3.3: Reactions of the Row Three Elements

Do you Remember? Complete the core - valence - radius diagrams below.

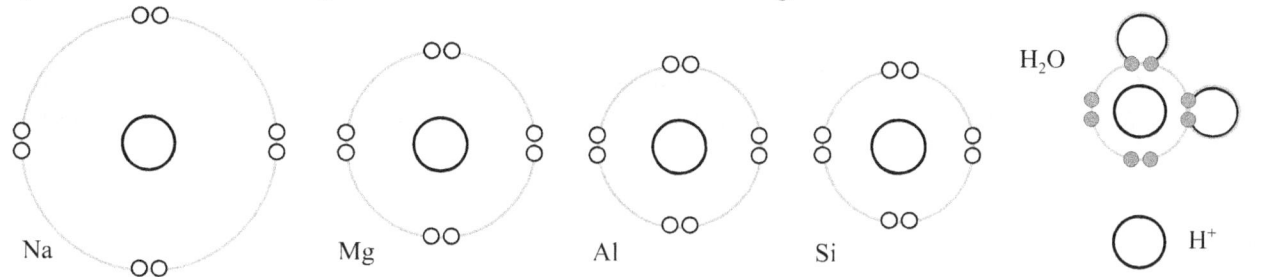

What's The Question? In the picture above, you can see how both the core charge and the atomic radius changes across a row of the periodic table. We will test the reactivity of each of these elements first with cold water, then with acid. (Acids contain the very small H^+ particles shown above. The H^+ particle is a hydrogen atom that has lost its only electron. All that is left is the positive core: a proton.)

What Are We Thinking About? **Caution: Danger of Fire, Caustic Products.** Sodium is dangerous to touch, and reacts explosively with water. Hydrochloric acid can injure eyes, skin, and damage clothing. *Never take your goggles off during this lab. Even if you finish, others may still be working.*

What Are We Doing?

Part A: Reactivity of elements with water.

1. Obtain small pieces of sodium, magnesium, aluminum and silicon.

2. Clean 4 small beakers, and put 20 mL of cold water into each one.

3. Put the sodium in the first beaker, magnesium in the second, aluminum in the third, and silicon in the fourth. Record your observations.

4. Pour out the water, but **keep the unreacted metals**. If your metal samples have already reacted in part A, *don't* get more metal.

Part B: Reactivity with Hydrochloric Acid

5. Put 10 mL of dilute hydrochloric acid into each beaker that still contains unreacted elements.

6. Record your observations.

7. Clean up the beakers, and return any unused elements to the front bench.

© Ross Lattner Publishing   www.rosslattner.ca

... of the Ross Periodic Table

Name:
Date:

Focus Question: Write the question that you are trying to answer.

1 **Predict** the order of activity with water, from most reactive to least reactive. Predict the order of activity with acid.	2 **Explain** your predictions, using the core - valence - radius diagrams and sentences.
3 **Observe** the reactivity of the row three elements with water and with acid, and record your observations here.	4 **Explain** your observations, using core - valence - radius diagrams, and sentences.

Questions For Later...

1. Phosphorus is the element between silicon and sulfur. It is missing from this experiment. Look up phosphorus on the internet, and explain why we did not include it in this experiment.

2. Would you expect calcium to be more or less reactive than potassium? Explain.

3. From which element(s) was water able to remove electrons? What evidence do you have?

4. From which element(s) was hydrochloric acid able to remove electrons? What evidence?

Table Manners
Student Exercises
Well Behaved Elements ...

Lab 3.4: Reactivity of the Noble Gases

Do you Remember? Complete the core - valence - radius diagrams at right.

Tungsten can be considered to have 6 valence electrons, and a core charge of +6.

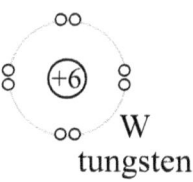
W
tungsten

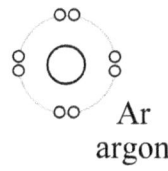
Ar
argon

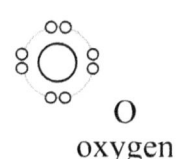
O
oxygen

What's The Question? An ordinary light bulb is filled with argon gas when it is manufactured.

Why do engineers fill the bulb with argon, and not with ordinary air?

What Are We Thinking About?

- The pressure of the argon gas in the bulb is about 80% of ordinary atmospheric pressure, a little less than the air pressure around you. It's certainly not a vacuum.

- The air around you contains 19% oxygen, 79% nitrogen, and about 1% argon. The remaining 1% is water, carbon dioxide and other gases.

- When the bulb is lit up, the tungsten filament is about 2 800 °C. Tungsten atoms can evaporate off the filament. The argon is included to bounce the tungsten particles back to the filament.

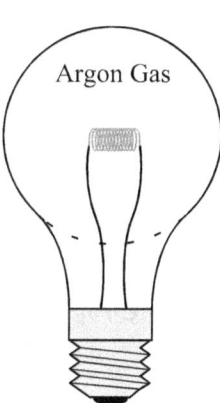
Argon Gas

What Are We Doing? Because of the hazards, your teacher will conduct this activity as a demonstration.

1. Test a 100 W light bulb just to make sure that it works. Identify the part that the light appears to come from. Let the light bulb cool.

2. Put the bulb inside double clear plastic bags. , and use a safe method to crack the glass bulb. Remove the broken glass with needle-nose pliers. Be careful not to break the filament. Examine the tungsten filament using a magnifying glass or microscope.

3. Put the light back into a lamp socket, and cover it with a large beaker.

4. **Predict:** what will happen to the filament when it is turned on?

5. **Explain,** using the Ross concepts.

6. **Observe** the experiment. Make complete records.

7. **Explain** your observations, using the Ross models of O, W and Ar.

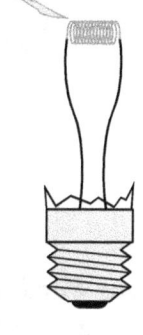
Tungsten filament

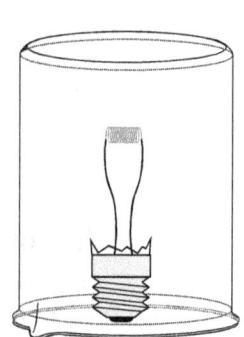

… **of the Ross Periodic Table**

Name:
Date:

Focus Question: Write the question that you are trying to answer.

1 Predict	2 Explain
3 Observe	4 Explain

Questions For Later...

1. Can *oxygen* take electrons away from tungsten? Give evidence for your answer.

2. Can *argon* take electrons away from tungsten? Give evidence for your answer.

3. One method of welding metals is TIG welding (Tungsten Inert Gas). A very hot electric spark from a tungsten wire melts the metal, and a stream of argon gas covers the hot metal. Explain why engineers chose tungsten and argon.

© Ross Lattner Publishing   www.rosslattner.ca

You can say something nice, dear, if you think long enough
How Good are your Table Manners?

Quiz 3: Well-Behaved Elements of the Core Valence Radius Table

---

1   Lithium, sodium and potassium react with water.

a) Label each element.

b) Write the core charge.

c) Add the valence electrons.

d) Which element is most reactive with water? Explain why.

Date: _____ / 5

---

1   Fluorine, chlorine and bromine are the reactive halogen elements.

a) Label each element.

b) Write the core charge.

c) Add the valence electrons.

d) Which element is most reactive with magnesium? Explain why.

Date: _____ / 5

---

3   (1.5, 1.8, 2.1)

Phosphorus, silicon and aluminum are very important elements.

a) Label each element.

b) Add core charge and valence electrons.

c) Which is the most reactive non-metal? Explain why.

Date: _____ / 5

4

Row 4 elements K, Ca, Ga, Ge and As

a) Label each element.

b) Add core charge and valence electrons.

c) Name any metalloids, and explain why you chose them.

Date: _____ / 5

© Ross Lattner Publishing   www.rosslattner.ca

You can say something nice, dear, if you think long enough
How Good are your Table Manners?

Quiz 3: Well-Behaved Elements of the Core Valence Radius Table   Name:

---

5 Mg and Ca are alkali earth elements.

a) Label each element.

b) Write the core charge.

c) Add the valence electrons.

d) Which one is most likely to lose a valence electron to chlorine? Explain.

Date: _____ / 5

---

6 The first three halogens are F, Cl, and Br.

a) Label each element.

b) Write the core charge.

c) Add the valence electrons.

d) Which one is most likely to tear a valence electron away from a metal? Explain.

Date: _____ / 5

---

7 Ar, Ne and He are noble gases.

a) Label each element.

b) Write the core charge.

c) Add the valence electrons.

d) Why are these elements used in situations that require a non-reactive substance? Explain fully.

Date: _____ / 5

---

8 Group 6 contains O, S, and Se..

a) Label each element.

b) Write the core charge.

c) Add the valence electrons.

d) Which of these elements is most likely to take electrons from Al? Explain fully.

Date: _____ / 5

© Ross Lattner Publishing   www.rosslattner.ca

Table Manners
Student Exercises

Electron Clouds ...

Activity 4.1: Covalent Bonds

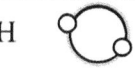 H

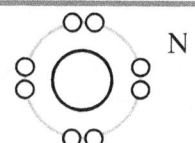 N

Do you Remember?

Complete the Ross diagrams for Phosphorus, Hydrogen, Nitrogen and Chlorine.

Write the electronegativity of each element.

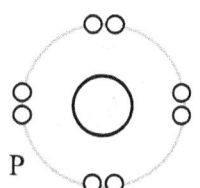 P

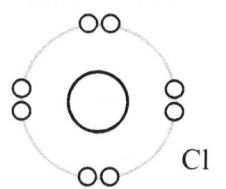 Cl

What's The Question? Molecules are made up of two or more atoms, held together by chemical bonds. *How do chemical bonds hold atoms together to make molecules?*

What Are We Thinking About?

- Electrons, which carry a negative charge, are attracted to the positive charge in the atomic core. But the attraction works both ways. Atomic cores are just as strongly attracted to electrons.

- Covalent bonds occur between two *non-metal* atoms. Non-metals have the large core charges and small radii, so they can attract and hold each others' electrons to make shared pairs of electrons.

What Are We Doing?
Consider two chlorine atoms. Both atoms have one vacancy on the valence shell. Both chlorines have one unpaired electron, very close to a +7 core charge. See the arrows.

Separate Chlorine atoms

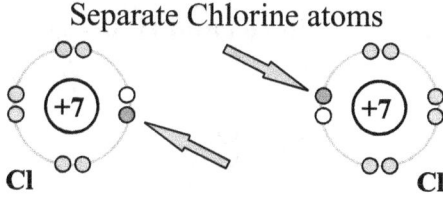

How could things be better for those electrons? They could get very close to *two* +7 core charges!

1. Re-draw the atoms so the unpaired electrons are attracted into the vacancy in the other chlorine atom's valence shell.

   Shared pair of valence electrons

   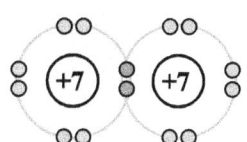

   The shared pair of electrons is strongly attracted to both +7 core charges. A covalent bond is a *shared pair of electrons that holds two atoms together*!

Complete the pairs of atoms to show the sharing of electrons, and the resulting covalent bond.

1. Hydrogen and Hydrogen. .	2. Fluorine and Fluorine. .
	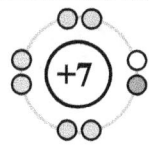 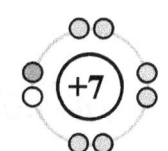

© Ross Lattner Publishing   75   www.rosslattner.ca

... and Chemical Bonding

Name:
Date:

Oxygen and nitrogen can share more than one pair of electrons, and form more than one covalent bond. Complete these examples to show how they could form double or triple bonds.

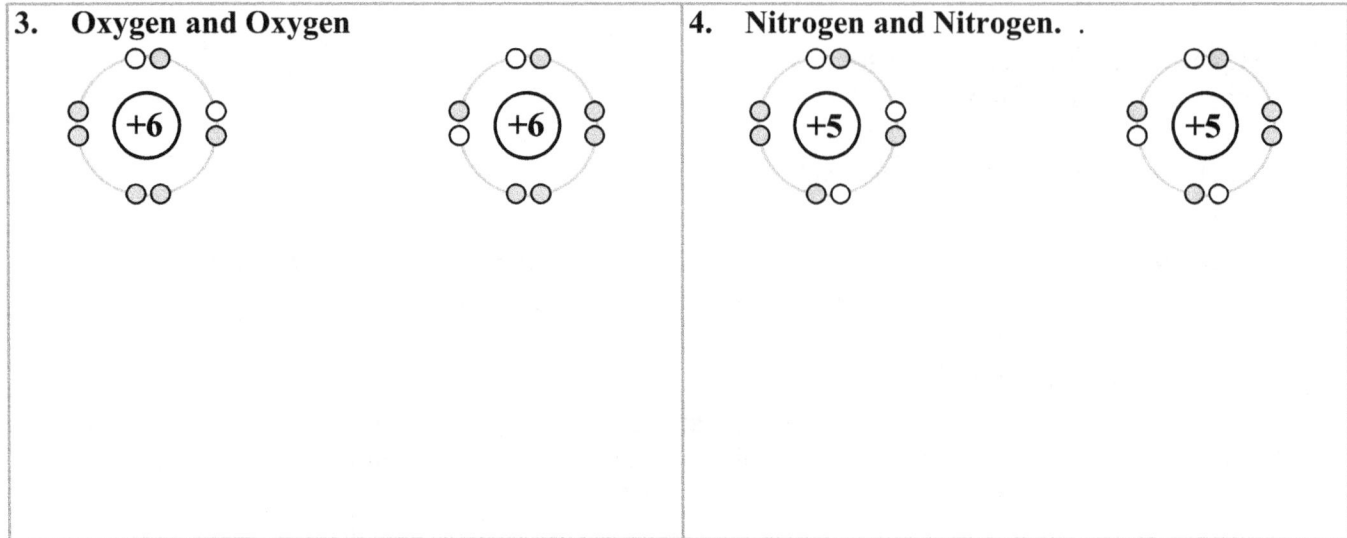

Compare the electronegativities of Phosphorus and Hydrogen. Would P and H be able to share electrons equally? How about Nitrogen and Chlorine? Draw the molecules, with the shared bonding pairs.

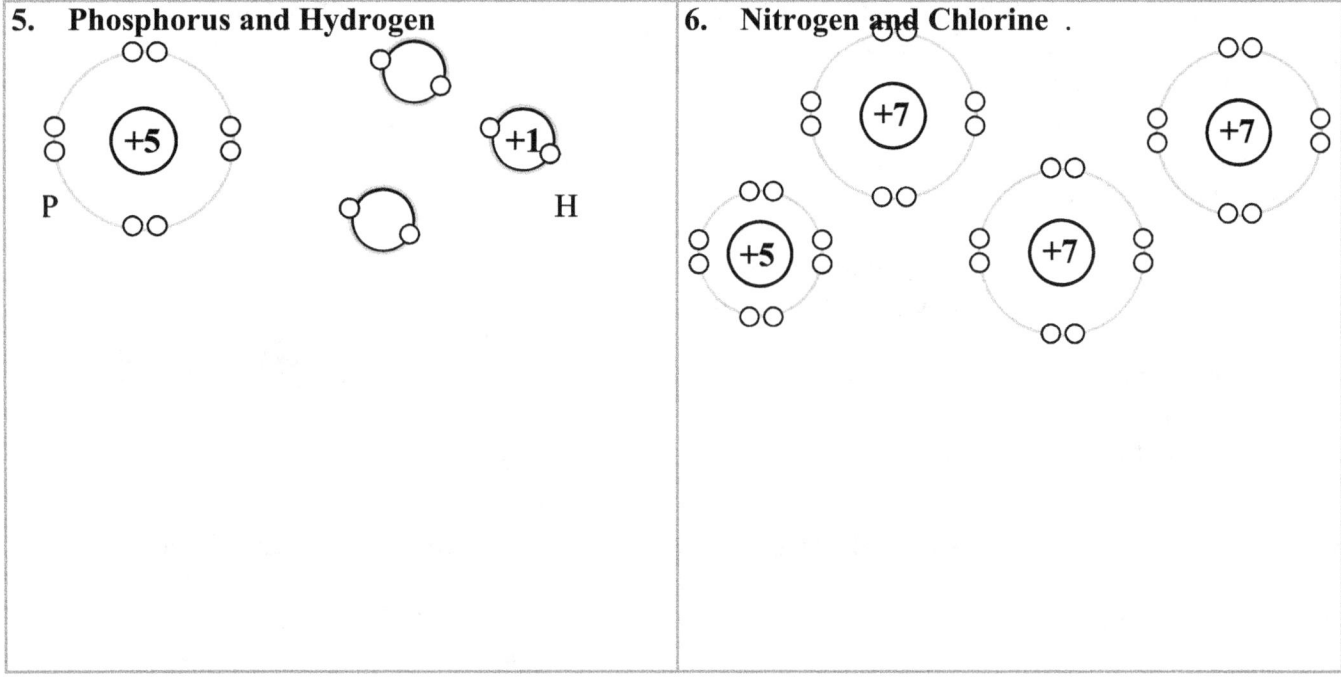

Questions for Later...

1. The chemical formula for water is H_2O. Draw Ross diagrams to show how H_2O is bonded.

2. Write the chemical formula for each of the molecules above.

© Ross Lattner Publishing   www.rosslattner.ca

Table Manners
Student Exercises

Electron Clouds ...

Activity 4.2: Polar Covalent Bonds
Do you Remember?

Complete the Ross diagrams for Fluorine, Nitrogen Carbon and Oxygen..

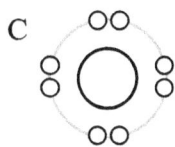
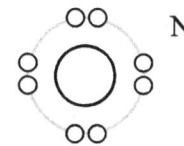

Write the electronegativity of each element.

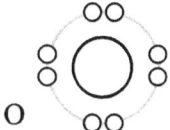
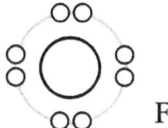

What's The Question?
Covalent bonds occur between atoms of non-metals. In most cases, the atoms are different from each other. *How do different kinds of non-metal atoms share electrons to make covalent bonds?*

What Are We Thinking About?
- Different non-metal atoms have different core charges, different radii, and therefore different electronegativities. They can share electrons, but they might not share them equally.

- The shared pairs of electrons will tend to spend more time around the greatest core charge.

- Shared pairs of electros will tend to spend more time around the smaller atom.

What Are We Doing?

Hydrogen and chlorine have one vacancy on the valence shell, and one unpaired electron.

1. Find the unpaired electrons and vacancies.

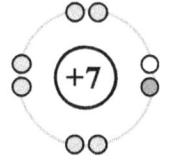

2. Re-draw the atoms to show that the covalent pair is shared unequally.

    The bonding electrons are more strongly attracted to chlorine than to hydrogen.

    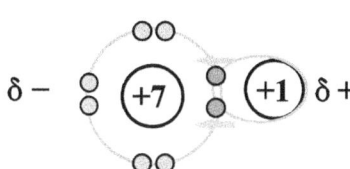

    This makes the bond polarized: the chlorine end of the bond is more negative than the hydrogen end.

© Ross Lattner Publishing   www.rosslattner.ca

... and Chemical Bonding

Name:
Date:

Complete these pairs of atoms to show the polar covalent bonds

1. Hydrogen and Fluorine .

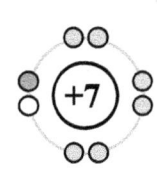 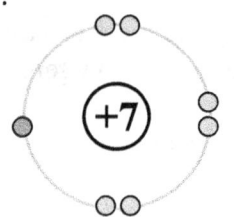

2. Fluorine and Bromine .

Atoms with more than one unpaired electron, or more than one vacancy, can form multiple bonds. Each bond can also be polar.. Complete these to show multiple polar covalent bonds.

3. Oxygen and Carbon

 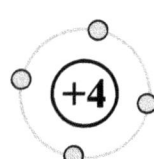 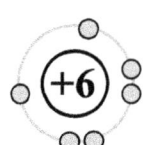

4. Nitrogen and Hydrogen. .

 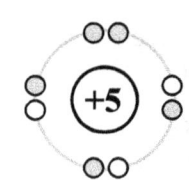 

Questions For Later...

1. In polar covalent bonds the shared pairs spend more time around the more electronegative atom. This moves the electron cloud toward the more electronegative atom. Mark the more positive atoms δ + and the more negative atoms δ - in each of the molecules above.

© Ross Lattner Publishing   www.rosslattner.ca

Table Manners
Student Exercises

Electron Clouds ...

Activity 4.3: Ionic Bonds

Do you Remember? Complete and label the Ross diagrams for Sodium and Fluorine. Use the words Large, Small, Many and Few to complete the blanks.

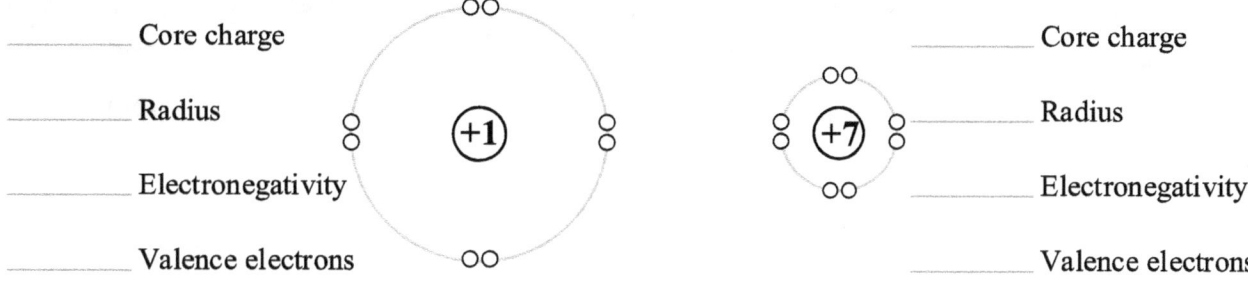

_____ Core charge

_____ Radius

_____ Electronegativity

_____ Valence electrons

_____ Core charge

_____ Radius

_____ Electronegativity

_____ Valence electrons

What's The Question? How do two elements bond together if they are very different? Metals and non-metals are radically different. *How do metals and non-metals bond together?*

What Are We Thinking About? The greater the differences between two people, the less likely that they can share something equally between them. Instead, the one will end up with the greater portion.

What Are We Doing?

1. Fluorine strongly attracts any electrons close to its valence shell. In this case, F attracts the single electron from Na right into its own valence shell. Fluorine now has custody of sodium's electron.

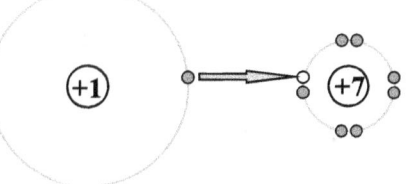

2. The weakly held Na electron has moved to the F atom, leaving the Na as nothing but the positive core, and the F with a negative charge.

3. The Na⁺ ion and the F⁻ ion attract each other, and can get closer to each other as ions than they could have as atoms.

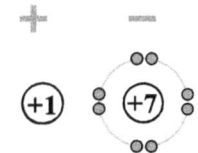

Complete these pairs of atoms.

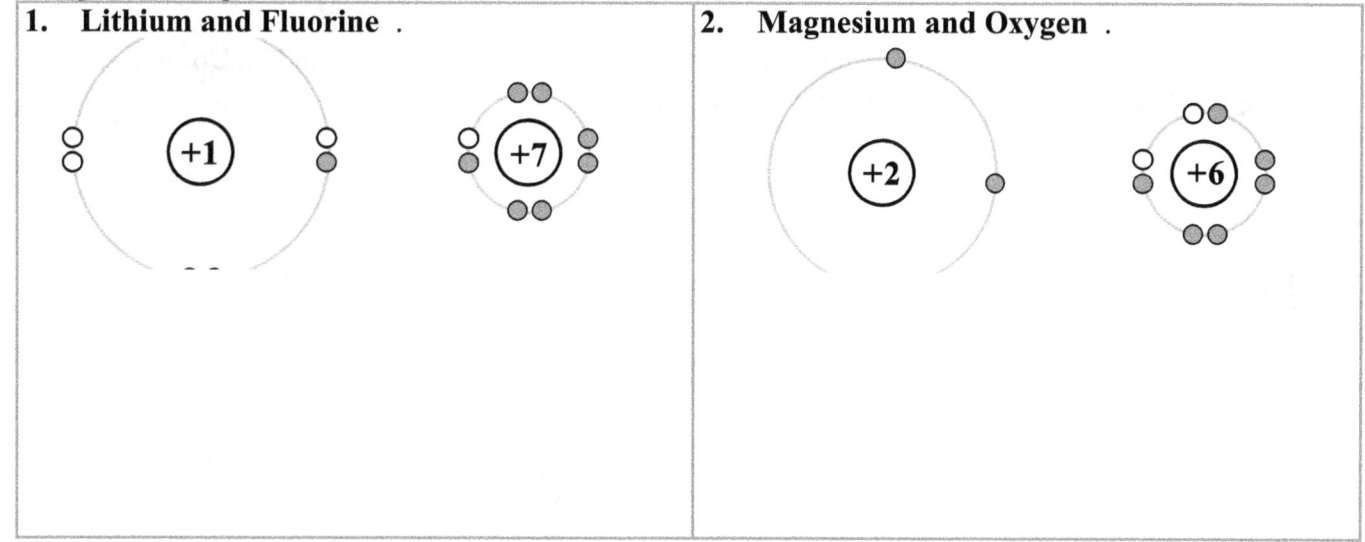

© Ross Lattner Publishing   www.rosslattner.ca

... and Chemical Bonding

Name:
Date:

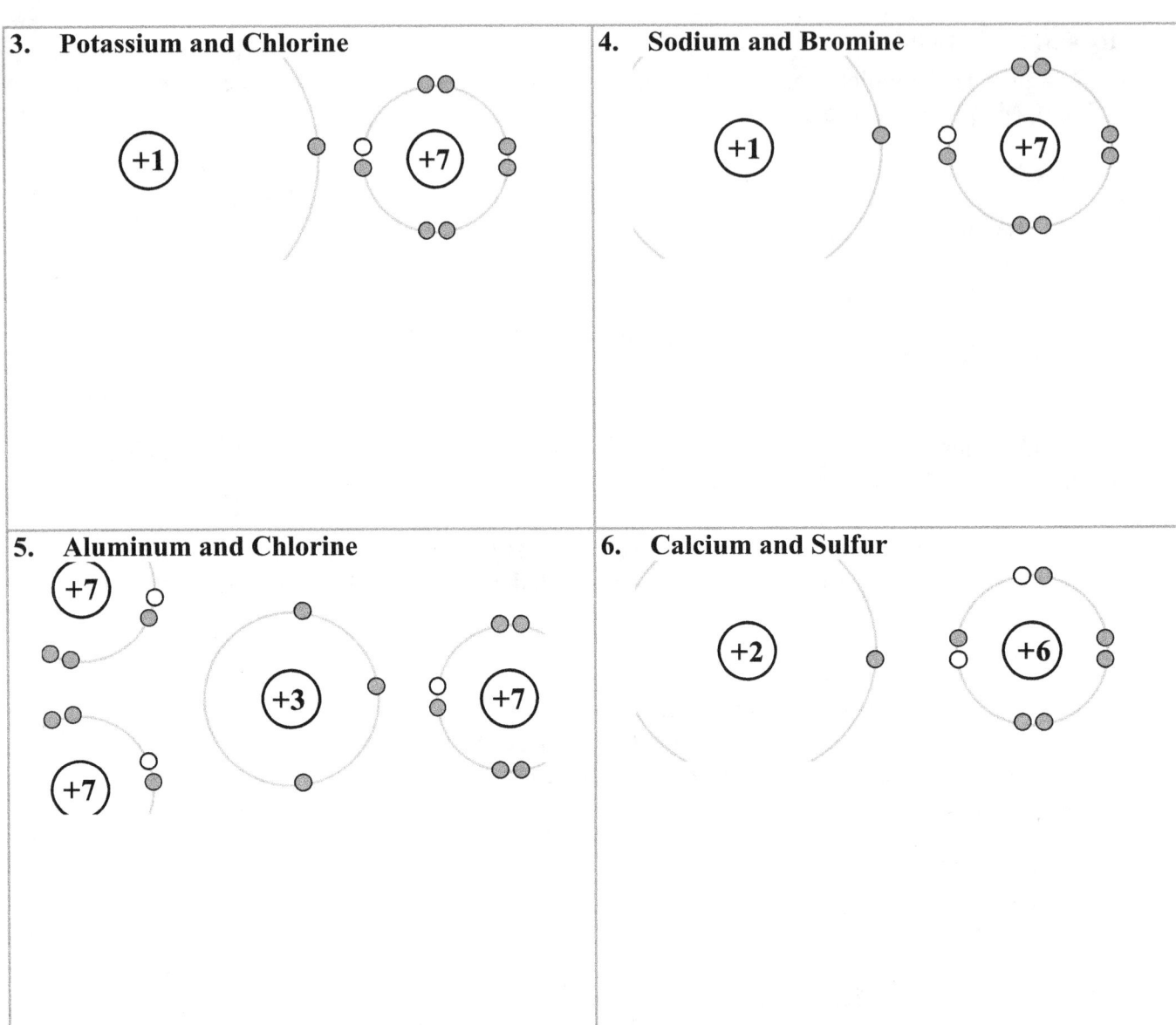

Questions For Later...

1. "Whenever a metal and a non-metal react, the product is an ionic compound." Do you agree or disagree with that statement? Explain your answer.

2. Rust is iron oxide. Is rust an ionic compound? Explain.

Table Manners
Student Exercises

Electron Clouds ...

Lab 4.4: Ionic Solids, Covalent Solids, and Network Solids

What's The Question? In this lab, you will test several solids for *odor*, *hardness*, and *melting point*.

What are the differences between solids composed of ionic crystals, solids made of covalent molecules, and the covalent network solids?

What Are We Doing? Obtain a cool hot plate, and clean it before you begin.

To test the melting point: Place a tiny crystal of each substance on a **cold** hot plate. You will have 7 different crystals on the hot plate at once. Plug the plate in, note the time at which each crystal melts. The longer the time, the higher the melting point.

To test hardness: crush one crystal between a scoopula and a glass plate. Judge hardness from the force with which the solid can be crushed.

To test odor: cautiously smell the mouth of the chemical jar by wafting a little air from the mouth of the jar toward your nose.

What Are We Thinking About?
1. *Ionic compounds* are formed from metals + non-metal. They form hard, gritty crystalline solids. (e.g. salt, chalk, baking soda, limestone, rust).

2. *Covalent compounds* are formed from non-metal + non-metal. These usually form small molecules. (e.g. water, sugar, oil, vinegar, wax).

3. *Covalent network compounds* are formed when non-metals atoms are linked into vast chains and networks. Usually really tough or hard. (e.g. diamonds, glass, quartz, mica, asbestos, nylon, hair, plastics).

Substance	Odor	Melting Point	Appearance	Hardness	Ionic or Covalent
Menthol					Covalent
Sodium Chloride					Ionic
Camphor					Covalent
Magnesium Bromide					Ionic
Silicon					Network
Unknown A					
Unknown B					

© Ross Lattner Publishing   www.rosslattner.ca

... and Chemical Bonding

Name:
Date:

Decide whether the following combination of elements will form ionic or covalent bonds. Then decide whether electrons will be transferred, or form shared pairs. Finally, draw the products as either an ionic crystal, a covalent molecule, or a covalent network solid.

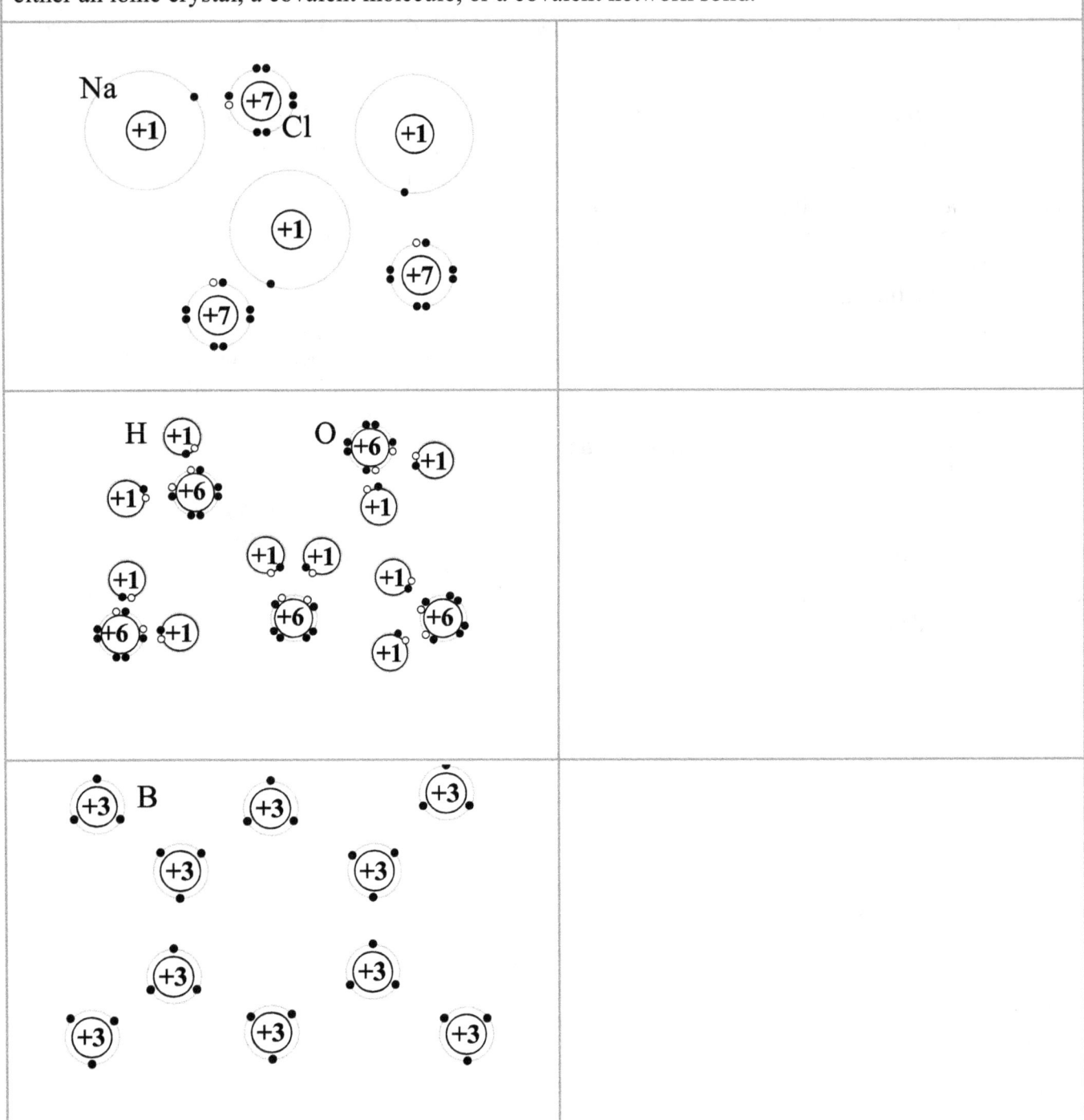

Questions For Later...

1. What generalization can you make about the melting point of ionic solids vs. covalent compounds?

2. What generalization can you make about the odor of ionic solids vs. covalent solids?

Table Manners
Student Exercises

Electron Clouds ...

Activity 4.5: Electron Clouds and Electron Density

Do you Remember? Complete the Ross diagrams for Sodium and Oxygen.

What's The Question? We know that electrons "fly around" the atom. Do they move quickly or slowly? Do they follow perfect circular orbits, or wobble all over the place?

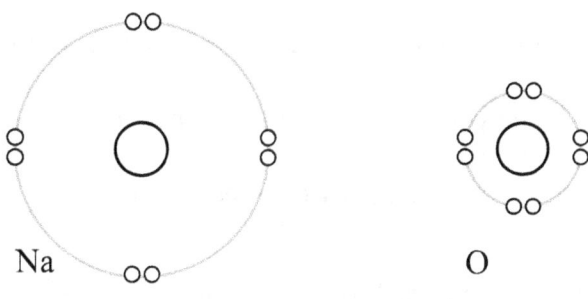

What would the motion of the electrons look like if we could see them?

What Are We Thinking About? Here are three analogies for the motion of an electron around an atomic core:

- An electron is like a marble moving in a bowl: sometimes it moves in a circle, but it usually changes speed and direction, sweeping down one side and up the other.

- An electron moves like a rubber stopper attached to an elastic band. The rubber stopper sometimes moves in a circular path, but often just "boings" from one side to the other. The stronger and shorter the elastic band, the faster the motion.

- Like a spinning fan blade, an electron is "smeared out" and fills a volume of space.

What Are We Doing? Imagine the electron, weakly attracted to a +1 core charge, and at a large radius from the core.

1. Obtain a colored marker or pencil.

2. Find one unpaired electrons on the atom, and place your marker on it.

3. Your colored marker (the electron) lazily wobbles around the core, tracing out long, slow, smooth, irregular curves.

4. Continue this for, say, 5 seconds. The result is a kind of map of the electron's location, observed over a period of time.

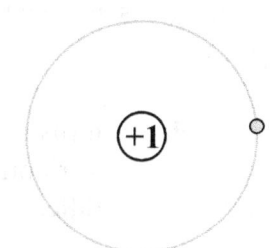

5. Now think of a chlorine atom. Its unpaired electron is closer to a much stronger core charge. Its motion would be much more rapid. Tracing out its path for 5 seconds yields a much denser electron cloud.

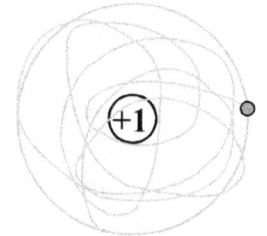

6. Electron density can be thought of as the concentration of electric charge in a region of space, something like the concentration of color in your picture.

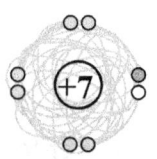

© Ross Lattner Publishing www.rosslattner.ca

... and Chemical Bonding

Name:
Date:

Each question deals with two atoms. Note the similarities and differences between the two atoms. Draw electron clouds around the atoms, that would reflect the differences in the two atoms.

1. **Oxygen and Carbon.** Label the two atoms.

   Place your colored marker or pencil on one electron, and trace the trajectory of the electron to indicate the electron densities around each atom.

2. **Oxygen and Sulfur** have the same core charge and valence electrons, but different radii. Identify and name the atoms.

   Repeat the exercise to indicate the different electron densities around the two atoms.

3. **Bromine and Aluminum** have similar radii, but very different core charges and valence shells.

   Show the electron densities, as before.

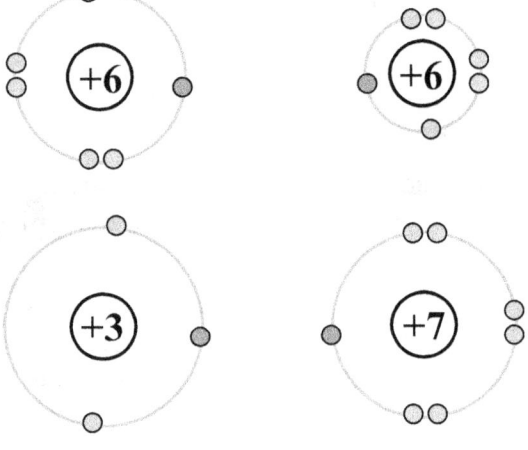

Covalent bonds are electron clouds too. The bonding electron clouds behave differently in different kinds of bonds.

Pure covalent bonds share the electrons equally. The electron cloud is spread over both atoms equally, but has the greatest density in the middle.

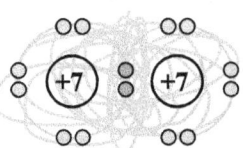

Polar covalent bonds share the bonding pair, but not equally. The electron cloud is distorted toward the more electronegative element. In hydrogen chloride, the hydrogen has little electron density around it.

The covalent bond has +,- poles.

δ+ (+1) (+7) δ−

Ionic bonds. In NaF, the electron can be thought of as spending practically all of its time around the F ion. There is a small chance that it flits over to the Na+ ion as well. You can think of this as a very extreme form of a polar covalent bond, with whole positive and negative charges.

+   (+1)   (+7)   −

© Ross Lattner Publishing   www.rosslattner.ca

You can say something nice, dear, if you think long enough

How Good are your Table Manners?

Quiz 4: Covalent, Polar and Ionic Bonding

---

1. Bromine, Br_2 is a dark red-brown liquid at room temperature. Draw Ross diagrams to show the covalent bonding of the two Br atoms.

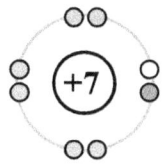 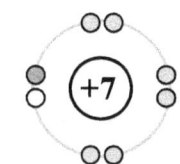

Date: _____ / 5

---

2. Hydrogen sulfide H_2S, is a toxic, smelly gas that is given off by rotten eggs and swamps. Are the H_2S bonds pure covalent, or polar covalent? Explain.

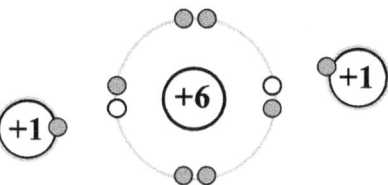

Date: _____ / 5

---

3. Calcium chloride, $CaCl_2$, is used in road construction in the summer to suppress dust. Is $CaCl_2$ covalent, or ionic? Show the bonding.

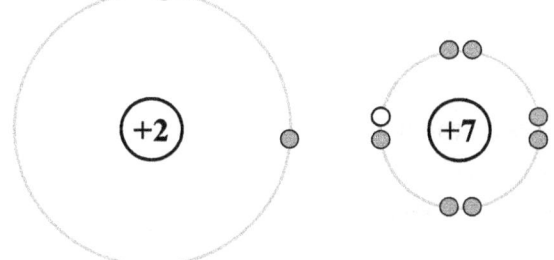

Date: _____ / 5

---

4. Decide whether water, H_2O, is pure covalent, polar covalent, or ionic, and draw the bonding using Ross diagrams.

 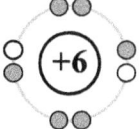

Date: _____ / 5

You can say something nice, dear, if you think long enough
How Good are your Table Manners?

Quiz 4: Covalent, Polar and Ionic Bonding   Name:

---

5 Hydrogen chloride, HCl, is a pungent gas that dissolves in water to make hydrochloric acid. Decide what kind of chemical bond exists between H and Cl. Draw Ross diagrams to show the bonding between hydrogen and chlorine.

6 Decide whether KBr will form ionic or covalent bonds. Draw the products as either an ionic crystal or a covalent molecule.

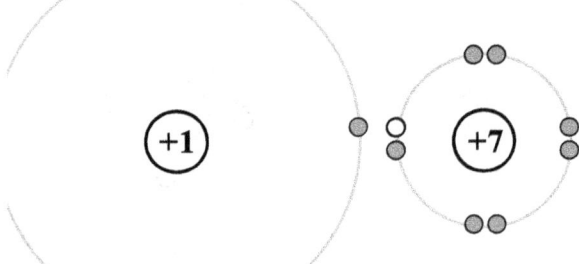

Date: / 5   Date: / 5

---

7 When hydrochloric acid reacts with a magnesium, H_2 hydrogen gas is produced. Is H_2 ionic, polar covalent, or pure covalent? Draw Ross diagrams to show the bonding.

8

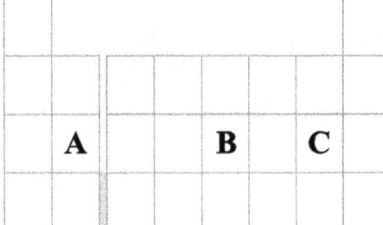

Which two atoms will combine to make:

____ & ____   an ionic compound

____ & ____   a polar covalent compound

____ & ____   a pure covalent compound

NB... You may use each letter more than once.

Date: / 5   Date: / 5

© Ross Lattner Publishing   www.rosslattner.ca

> You can say something nice, dear, if you think long enough
> # *How Good are your Table Manners?*

Quiz 4: Covalent, Polar and Ionic Bonding   Name:

9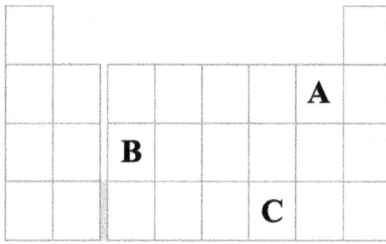

what kind of bond would form between:

B & A   _____

C & A   _____

A & A   _____

Date: _____   / 5

10   Ammonia is a very smelly compound composed of nitrogen and hydrogen. Show how these molecules can become 2 molecules of ammonia, NH_3.

Date: _____   / 5

11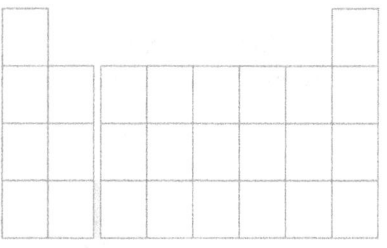

Mark the correct boxes with Ca, H, and P.

Would Ca and H form a covalent or ionic compound? Give reasons.

Would H and P form a covalent or ionic compound? Give reasons.

Date: _____   / 5

12   Carbon and sulfur form the compound CS_2.

a)   What kind of bond would form between carbon and sulfur? Give reasons.

b)   Draw Ross diagrams of the bonding.

Date: _____   / 5

© Ross Lattner Publishing   www.rosslattner.ca

You can say something nice, dear, if you think long enough
How Good are your Table Manners?

Quiz 4: Covalent, Polar and Ionic Bonding   Name:

---

13 Iodine, I_2, forms dark purple crystals. Place your pen on one of the bonding electrons, and trace a possible trajectory for that electron to show the location of the bonding electron cloud.

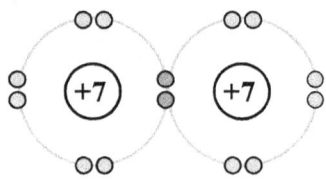

Is this bond polar? Explain.

Date: / 5

---

14 Hydrogen iodide is a colorless gas. Place your pen on one of the bonding electrons, and trace a possible trajectory for that electron to show the location of the bonding electron cloud.

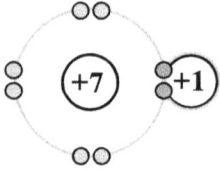

Is this bond polar? Explain.

Date: / 5

---

15 Common chlorine bleach, the kind you buy in the grocer store, contains hypochlorous acid, HOCl.

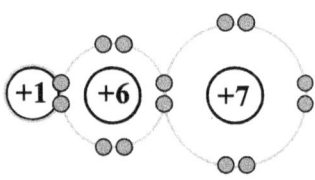

Place your pen on one of the bonding electrons between H and O, and trace a possible trajectory for that electron to show the location of the bonding electron cloud. Repeat for Cl and O.

Which atom has the greatest electron density?

Date: / 5

---

16 Methanol is a toxic alcohol used in windshield washer fluid.

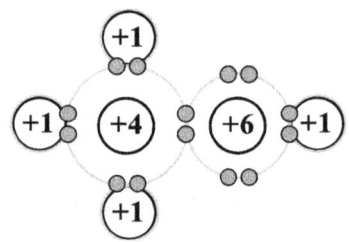

Trace possible trajectories for one bonding electron from each bonding pair, to show the location of the bonding electron cloud.

Which bond has the greatest dipole character?

Date: / 5